Getting St

Java A

CW01085790

Another book
by
Owen Bishop

BP554 Getting Started in *Java*

Getting Started with *Java* Applets

by

Owen Bishop

**BERNARD BABANI (publishing) LTD
THE GRAMPIANS
SHEPHERDS BUSH ROAD
LONDON W6 7N
ENGLAND**

www.babanibooks.com

Please Note

Although every care has been taken with the production of this book to ensure that any projects, designs, listings, etc., contained herewith, operate in a correct and safe manner and also that any downloads specified are freely available on the World Wide Web, the Publisher and Author do not accept responsibility in any way for the failure (including fault in design) of any projects, designs, or listings to work correctly or to cause damage to any equipment that may be used, or in respect of any other damage or injury that may be so caused, nor do the Publishers accept responsibility in any way for the failure to obtain specified downloads.

© 2006 BERNARD BABANI (publishing) LTD

First Published — September 2006

British Library Cataloguing in Publication Data
A catalogue record for this book is available from the British Library

ISBN 0 85934 562 9

Cover Design by Gregor Arthur

Printed and Bound in Great Britain by Cox & Wyman Ltd, Reading.

About the author

Owen Bishop is well known as a contributor to popular computing and electronics magazines and is the author of over 75 books, mostly in computing, electronics, and robotics. His talent for introducing technical subjects to beginners is proven by the many successful books he has written.

Acknowledgements

The *Stunt Car* program in chapter 11 is the *Java* version of a BBC BASIC program by Audrey Bishop (*Take Off with the Electron and BBC Micro*, Granada Publishing 1984).

The *Sniper* program in chapter 11 is the *Java* version of a BBC BASIC program by Owen and Audrey Bishop (*The Commodore64 Games Book*, Granada Publishing 1983).

Thanks are due to granddaughters Emma and Laura Bishop for testing many of the applets.

Trademarks

Java is the registered trademark of Sun Microsystems Inc. *Windows XP* is the registered trademark of Microsoft Corporation. The term Windows, as used in this book, refers to Microsoft Windows.

Contents

Why and how to use this book

Applets are short programs written in *Java*. They are widely used to add interest and excitement to web pages, but can also be run off-line. If you would like to know more, read on.

This is a book for beginners. It is for those who wonder what *Java* is about. It is for those of us who like to get to grips with their computer rather than use it at arm's length by running commercially produced software.

Above all, it is for those who enjoy hands-on and thoughts-on computing. For those who want to have fun.

The applets in this book are short and intended to illustrate what can be done with the *Java* language. They will help you to become familiar with frequently used *Java* terms and techniques. From here you may want to progress to the massive handbooks we find on the 'Computing' shelves of bookshops. We decided to go for applets rather than write application programs because each applet can be relatively compact, easily understood, and easily run on the free Applet Viewer software.

What will you do with these applets after you have typed them in and possibly enhanced and customised some of them? For a start, you will learn something from using them. If you have a website, put your best applets on web pages and share them with friends.

If some of your best applets happen to be games, put them on your laptop and enjoy running them off-line on the way to work.

The book is divided into three parts.

Part One covers the essential stages of writing applets and testing and viewing them, either off-line or on the web. There is a discussion about the relative merits of using the original *Java 1* or the more powerful, but more complicated, *Java 2* methods. Part 1 ends by guiding you to some web sites that carry useful information about applets and related topics.

Part Two has listings that illustrate many aspects of *Java* in general and applets in particular. But these are not intended to be just typed in, run a few times, and then forgotten. Look at them as starting points from which you develop something more polished. It may have added facilities. It may be customised to produce an applets that reflects your requirements — and, perhaps, your personality.

Part Three contains reference material. The first section is *Java Digest*. You need to have a smattering of *Java* in order to understand the applet listings in Part 2. There are several introductions to the language, including the author's *Getting Started in Java* (Babani Computing Books BP554). In this Part we present a summary of the Java methods and techniques that you will find most useful when studying our applets and when creating your own. This is backed up by a series of eleven *Digest applets*. These are workbenches for testing out the actions of the methods practically.

The **Finding the class** and **Finding the method** sections of Part Three lead you to the applet classes that are detailed in the book, and to the working examples of the many *Java* methods described.

1 Creating applets

An applet is a computer application written in the *Java* language. Usually it is short. The most important thing about it is that applets are often found embedded in pages on a website.

The pages of a website are normally written in a language called *Hyper-Text Mark-up Language* (or *HTML* for short). But the *HTML* pages may also include applets, which are written in *Java*. So, why include applets?

Applets can do things that are not available in *HTML*. For example, they can generate animated graphics, and are able to download information. The usefulness of applets for enhancing web pages has made *Java* one of the most popular of computer languages.

Another language used to improve web pages is *Javascript*. But this is entirely different from *Java*, even though their names are similar. *Javascript* lacks the power of *Java*. It is not used for applets, and we shall not discuss it further in this book.

We assume in this book that the reader already knows a little *Java*. If you need a simple introduction to the language, see the author's *Getting Started in Java* (BP554). It has a chapter on applets but now we take this topic and look into many more aspects of it.

Downloading *Java*

At the time of writing, the *Java* software is available for downloading free of charge from the website of Sun Microsystems Inc, the originators of the language. Their URL is:

http://java.sun.com

Follow the instructions on the screen to download *J2SE* (*Java 2 Standard Edition*). At the time of writing, the latest version of this is 1.50, sometimes known as *Tiger*. This is the version on which this book is based.

In PCs, *Java* is run from a command line, that is, in the same way as running a DOS program. If your computer is running *Windows 95, 98, NT* or *2000*, click on the MS-DOS icon to obtain the DOS screen. In *Windows XP*, reach the command line by first clicking on the 'Start' button at the bottom left of the screen. Then click 'Run'. When the small 'Run' window appears, type 'cmd' (without the quotes) and click on OK.

In the DOS or command line window, the lowest line contains text beginning with 'C:\'. This indicates that you are working in the root directory of the computer, on Drive C.

You may find that there is other text following the 'C:\', such as the name of one of the folders saved on your hard disc. If so, you are at present working in a sub-directory. You need to get back to the root directory, which comprises the whole of your hard disc, drive C. Do this by typing 'CD ..' and press Enter. The letters 'CD' mean 'change directory' and the two full-stops mean 'to the next higher directory'. Do not forget to leave a space after 'CD'. If you were in a sub-directory, of a sub-directory, of a sub-directory of the root directory to begin with, type 'CD ..' followed by the 'Enter' key several times.

Eventually, only 'C:\' appears on the lowest screen line. This shows that you are now working in the root directory. The next and final step is to type in the pathway to the sub-directory (or folder) in which your *Java* programs are stored.

4

Fig. 1 shows the stages in getting back to the root directory and then to the sub-directory in which the executable *Java* files are held. The exact path may be slightly different on your computer. In the example, we are running version 1.5.0 of *Java 2*, which is in the 'bin' subdirectory of the 'jdk1.5.0_01' subdirectory. This is in the 'Java' subdirectory of the 'Program files' directory. Sun has issued updated versions of *Java* which, at the time of writing, have reached 'jdk1.5.0_06'.

To navigate from the root to sub-directory 'bin' we use 'CD', but this time followed by the sub-directory names, separated by backslashes (see p. 7). You should use the names of whatever subdirectories *Java* has installed itself. The screen is shown in Fig. 1 as it should be when the computer is waiting for further instructions, to compile or run a *Java* program.

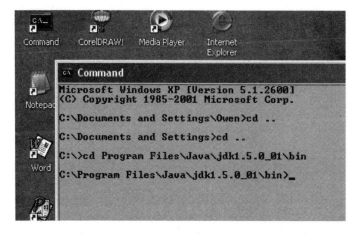

Fig. 1. This shows the stages of getting to the root directory and, from there, to the directory containing the main Java *files.*

Writing, compiling and running

We shall give fuller details on these topics in the next chapter, but this outline introduces the main stages in creating and testing applets.

There are three stages.

- **Writing:** The first stage is to write the applet, using simple text editing software, such as *WordPad* or *Notepad*. If you have a PC running *Windows* software, one or both of these programs are provided with it. *Notepad* saves text as simple text files, with no embedded formatting. *WordPad* can also save text in other formats, such as Rich Text Format. This includes non-printing codes for formatting the text. If you save your applet text in one of these other formats, you will receive dozens of error messages as *Java* tries to make sense of the codes in the file. When you save the file, always select 'Text Document' in the 'Save as type:' box at the bottom of the 'Save as...' window. Always type the filename with the extension '.java', not 'txt'.

- **Compiling:** When you have written part or the whole of an applet and, after you have inspected it for obvious errors, you use a program called *javac* to compile it. This turns your text into a coded version that *Java* can understand. While it is compiling your text, *javac* is busily scanning it for errors. As it finds these, it prints a list of them on the screen. These are known as **compile-time errors**. To correct compile-time errors, you need to return to the original text to locate and correct the errors, then re-compile the text using *javac*. Successful, error-free compiling produces a file with the same filename as your original text, but with the extension '.class'.

- **Running:** Finally, run the class file, using the applet viewer or a browser. How to use these is described in Chapter 2. The applet may run perfectly at this stage but occasionally there is something in the structure of the program that produces one or more **run-time errors**. You should not expect to have many of these. The *Java* program reports these on the screen and stops running the applet. To correct run-time errors, you need to return to the original text to locate and correct the errors, then re-compile the text using *javac*. Finally, run the viewer or browser to interpret the newly-compiled '.class' file.

This completes the three-stage sequence.

Backslash

If your keyboard is set to English (United Kingdom), you may find that you get a hash (#) when you press the backslash (\) key. To get a backslash, press *and hold* the Alternate (ALT) key *and* the F1 key while you type 092 on the *numeric keypad*. Release the ALT and F1 keys and a backslash will appear. Note that this does not work if you key 092 using the number keys above the QWERTY keys.

Display colours

By default, the command line window displays light grey text on a black background. You may be satisfied with this — in some ways it makes you feel 'near' to the computer's operations. But you can have other colours if you prefer.

The exact technique for altering the colours depends on the computer. For *Windows XP*, display the command line window as previously instructed. Then move the cursor to the title bar at the top of the command window and *right-click*. From the drop-down menu, select 'Defaults', which displays a window titled 'Console Windows Properties'. Click on the 'Screen text' button, then on one of the colours displayed below it. Click on the 'Screen background', then select a contrasting colour from the display. A small window shows the 'Selected screen colors', so you can see the effect.

For writing this book we chose yellow text on a blue background, which gives a cheerful and legible display. For the screen shots we chose black text on a light grey background, which prints out better on paper. You can try out various combinations before clicking on the 'OK' button to activate your choice. Of course, you can always come back again later and select new colours.

2 Viewing applets

It is traditional in books like this to begin by writing a program to display a short message. This book is no exception but, instead of the usual "Hello World!" greeting, we are boosting applets by declaring "Applets Are Awesome!".

Here is the applet that generates the text:

```
import java.applet.*;
import java.awt.*;

public class text extends Applet {

public void init() {

this.add(new Label("Applets are awesome!"));

}}
```

If you already know a bit of *Java*, this program is easy for you. Jump straight on to the next heading, on p. 10. If you are not quite sure of your *Java*, the next few pages explain how this applet works.

The listing begin by importing two *Java* packages, *java.applet* and *java.awt*. We also need the *java.lang* package but this is imported by default each time we run a *Java* program so we do not need to specify it by name. The *java.lang* package contains all the basic routines for a *Java* program. As you might guess, the *java.applet* package contains special methods required for running applets. The *java.awt* package contains the methods of the **abstract windowing toolkit,** for displaying buttons, pull-down menus, labels and many other visual efects.

Note the asterisk in each import command — the 'wild card' symbol. This means that we are importing *all* the methods in the package, not just one or a few. Note too the semicolons at the end of each statement. These are essential at the end of each program line in which the computer is told to DO something.

The definition of the class that is to produce the applet begins with the line:

```
public class text extends Applet {
```

The important word is 'class' indicating that this line begins the definition of a class. The term 'public' tells the computer that other *Java* classes are allowed access to this class. This makes sense because, if the class is not public, we should not be able to run it. The word 'text' is the name we have decided to give to this applet, to distinguish it from other applets that we shall write.

The words 'extends Applet' shows that there is already a class, called *Applet,* which contains the basic applet routines. The text class extends this by telling *Applet* what particular message to display on the screen. Then comes the class description, beginning with an opening curly bracket.

The description consists only of a definition of a method called *init()*. Note the pair of round brackets, indicating that *init()* is a method. This is going to set up the applet to display the text we have chosen. It is a public method, accessible from any other method, and the term 'void' means that it does not return any values for use in other methods.

9

Now, at last, we come to the line that tells the computer what to do. Left to itself, the *init()* method would display a blank white area on the screen and there would be no text. The action of the applet is to add a new Label to this method (the *init()* method). The text of the label is typed inside double quotes to indicate that is it a string. This string is passed across to the method as a **parameter**, by enclosing it in round brackets.

The line ends with a semicolon because it it a DOing line.

Preparing the class file

Run a simple text processor program, such as *Notebook*. Type in the listing exactly as on p. 8. Save it in the same 'bin' folder as used for all the other *Java* files. Its filename **must** be exactly the same as the name already used in line 3 of the listing, in this case, *text*. The extension of the filename **must** be *.java,* and not *.txt.*

Here is what to do:

Call up the command line screen as described on pp. 4-5. Navigate to the 'bin' folder. At the prompt (where the underline cursor is flashing) type:

```
javac text.java
```

After pressing Enter there is a delay of a second or two while the program is compiled. If there are no errors in the typing of *text.java*, the prompt reappears and waits for the next entry. If there are typing errors, one or more error messages are displayed. In a typical programming session you may be told about other kinds of error too but, as this listing has already been tested and found to work, there should be no errors other than typing errors.

The compiler *javac* has now produced a file of the same name (*text*) but with the extension *.class*. If this was a normal application file you could run it now, using the *java* program. However, applets are intended to be displayed in the window of a browser. We must now prepare a file that creates a browser window and displays the applet in it.

HTML pages

When we receive an e-mail or visit a site on the Web, the information is sent to the computer as a special kind of file. This is written in a language called *Hyper-Text Mark-up Language*, or *HTML* for short. Filenames have the extension *.html,* sometimes *.htm.*

HTML is essentially a language for formatting text, but it can handle images as well. Browsers such as *Internet Explorer* are able to use the directions given in an *HTML* file to create a screenful of coloured text and images.

The *HTML* file may also contain what is called 'active content'. This may call on short programs that are sent to your computer along with the *HTML* file. *Java* applets are examples of active content. Active-X controls are another example. So let us look at an *HTML* file with active content:

```
<HTML>
<HEAD>
<TITLE> Looking at Applets</TITLE>
</HEAD>

<BODY BGCOLOR = red>
<H1>Looking at Applets</H1>
<P>
<APPLET CODE=text WIDTH=250 HEIGHT=150>
</APPLET>
</BODY>
</HTML>
```

The active content begins at <APPLET CODE= ...

The instructions in an *HTML* program are written as **tags**. These are words and abbreviations enclosed in a pair of angled brackets. Examples in the file above are <HTML> and <H1>. The <HTML> tag tells the browser that everything that follows is an *HTML* file and must be acted on accordingly. The browser follows the instuctions in the file until it comes to the cancelling tag at the end, </HTML>.

Similarly, the <H1> tag tells the browser to display all the text that follows in the largest size of a standard heading. It does this until it come to the cancelling tag, </H1>.

You can use the following *HTML* program to display all the applets in this book, and there is no real need for you to understand and write *HTML* programs. However, most people like to be aware of what is going on, so here is an explanation of the HTML program.

As already explained, it begins with the <HTML> tag. The program always comes in two parts, head and body, so the next tag is <HEAD>. This simply contains a title for the page, prefaced by <TITLE> and followed by </TITLE>. That ends the head section, so next comes the closing tag, </HEAD>.

The body begins with the <BODY> tag. This is followed by an instruction that sets the background colour of the screen to red. This makes it easy to pick out the applet, which will have a white background. HTML has several basic colours that are called up by name. Blue, lime, and teal are examples that you can try.

The first item in the body is the heading, displayed in the largest size available. The heading is enclosed between <H1> and </H1>. Then comes <P> which starts a new paragraph. <P> does not necessarily need a closing tag.

The next 'paragraph' contains the applet. It begins with the <APPLET> tag, which also contains information about the applet. CODE is the filename of the class program, *text.class*, produced by *javac*. Note that we do not include the .class extension in the HTML file. The applet tag also includes the size of the screen area to be allocated to the applet. This is in pixels.

Finally, the program is ended by closing all the tags that are still open: </APPLET>, </BODY>, and </HTML>.

Creating and running the HTML program

Type in the program as listed on p. 11. Take special care to include all the closing tags, with their slashes. The HTML error-checking routines of *Internet Explorer* are limited and a typing error may simply result in an odd-looking display.

12

Save the file in the same *bin* folder, along with all the other *Java* files, including, of course, *text.class*. We used *LookAtThis.html* for the filename. Unlike *Java* files, the filename under which an *HTML* program is saved does not have to be the same as in the title.

The next step is to run *Internet Explorer* (or other browser) *off-line*. The description which follows applies strictly to *IE*, but other browsers, such as *Netscape Browser*, may be expected to behave in a similar way. Run *IE* and type in the following address (or URL):

file:///C:/Program files/Java/jdk1.5.0_06/bin/LookAtThis.html

If you are using a *Java* update other than 06, type its number instead of '06'. Click on 'Go'. The page should appear after a few seconds, and look like this:

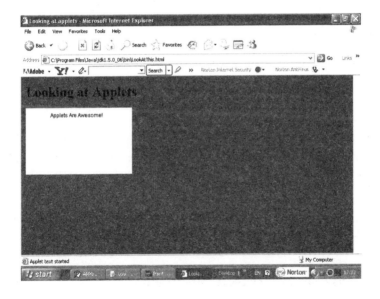

Fig. 2. The HTML *page,* LookAtThis, *displays the* text *applet.*

Security

If you are running the newer versions of *IE* you may find that the applet does not appear. You get just a red screen with the heading 'Looking at Applets' at the top. At the same time, a message appears at the top of the screen. This tells you that *IE* has detected active content in the *HTML* file and is blocking it. Click on this message and a small drop-down menu appears. Click on 'Allow blocked content'. There is a security warning to clear and then the applet appears after a delay of a few seconds.

If you are a cautious person, you may prefer to click on 'What's the risk?' If you do, a Help display explains about Active-X controls and possibly harmful code that the *HTML* file contains. When working on-line, it is true that a page *may* contain harmful code, especially a page written by someone you do not know. You have to decide whether or not to allow it. However, *Java* is well-known to be a very secure language, so there should be nothing to worry about. Click on 'Allow blocked content', click on 'Yes' at the warning, and see your first applet appear on the screen.

The Applet Viewer

This is another off-line technique for viewing applets. The applet appears in its own window. This technique is a quick one, suitable for developing new applets. But eventually you will want your applets to run in web pages and you will need to test them in a browser running off-line, as already described.

The *Applet Viewer* comes as part of the *Java* software downloaded from Sun Microsystems. To use it, you need an applet .class file and an *HTML* file containing the CODE reference to the .class file. Run the command screen and, at the prompt, type:

```
appletviewer LookAtThis.html
```

'appletviewer' is one word. Key 'Enter' and, in a second or two, the applet appears at the top left of the screen (see Fig. 3, opposite). Only the applet is seen. The *HTML* content of the file is not displayed.

14

In Fig. 3, the window has been dragged away from the top left corner to reveal the text on the command screen.

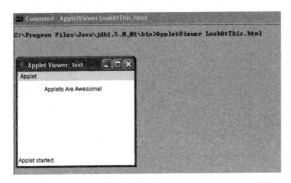

Fig. 3. Using the Applet Viewer from the command line prompt.

In Fig. 3, the applet is still running. You can tell this by noticing that the prompt has not reappeared on the next screen line. This reappears only when we close the applet by clicking on the 'X' at the top right corner of the applet window. The applet is then cleared from the screen.

Features of the viewer

The viewer has a drop-down menu, displayed by clicking on the 'Applet' button, located just above the display area (Fig. 4, overleaf).

The functions of the more often used options are:

- Restart: starts the applet again. Fig. 5 (overleaf) shows what happens.
- Reload: clears the applet from the screen, then runs it again. However the *init()* method is run only on the first run of a given session. No other methods are called in this applet, so it stays cleared and is not re-displayed.

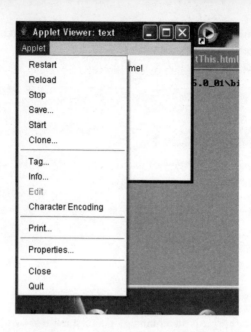

Fig. 4. The drop-down menu leads us to some useful features of the Applet Viewer.

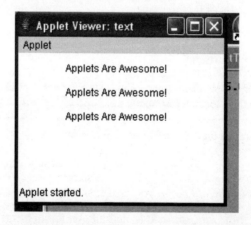

Fig. 5. The result of restarting the applet twice. Each time it calls on the init() *method, so the message appears a total of three times.*

16

- Clone: creates a copy of the applet. This can be kept on screen and handled independently.

- Tag: displays the line or lines in the *HTML* file that generate the applet.

- Print: prints out the listing of the applet.

- Close: closes the copy of the applet in which this option is selected, but not other copies.

- Quit: closes all copies of the applet, and the viewer, returning you to the command line.

HELP!

If you select 'reload' with an applet such as this, which has only an *init()* method, the display clears and you can not then select 'close' or 'quit' to end the applet. To get out of this difficulty, right-click on the Desktop bar, then click on 'Task Manager' in the displayed menu. This brings up the Task Manager window. Find *appletviewer.exe* in this window and click on it. Then click on the 'End Process' button at bottom right.

This stops the applet and returns you to the command line prompt.

ERRORS!

When you return to the command screen after experimenting with the *Applet Viewer*, you may often see a complex display of messages and warnings. These are usually the result of breaking off the applet before it has finished running, and can safely be ignored.

Combining the files

Instead of separate HTML and *Java* .class files, we can combine the two kinds into a single .class file. We simply include the HTML directions as a comment at the beginning of the .java file before the class definition begins. This is how to do it with the text applet:

```
import java.applet.*;
import java.awt.*;

/*
<APPLET CODE=text WIDTH=250 HEIGHT=150>
</APPLET>
*/

public class text extends Applet {

public void init() {

this.add(new Label("Applets Are Awesome!"));

}}
```

In this listing, the applet code has been inserted into the original *text.java* file, between the comment symbols, /* and */. Type this listing into *Notepad* and save it as text.java. Use *javac* to compile it as a text.class file. Run the program by typing:

```
appletviewer text.java
```

The applet appears at top left when you press 'Enter'. This procedure is the quicker to use when you are developing an applet. Remember that, if you want to call the applet directly by using the above command, the applet listing *must* include the applet code, because it tells *Java* the dimensions of the applet. You can add this code to other applet files from this book, if they do not have it already.

If you do not include the code, you need to call the applet from an HTML page, because the dimensions of the applet are in the HTML page (see pp. 12-13). Run the applet from the command line by typing:

```
appletviewer text.html
```

Or use a browser to run the HTML page, as previously described.

18

3 On the Web

Before you can put your applets on the World Wide Web you need two things:

- A website.
- Software for transferring files from your computer to your website.

The kind of website you need depends on how you intend to use it. Perhaps you just want to get started with applets. You can experience the fun of putting your home-brew applets on the website. You can share them with your friends and family by letting them know your site address.

In this case you will probably prefer to open a site hosted by the server that you already use for emailing and for access to the Web. Their home page will lead you to information about the kinds of site they can provide.

There may be several types on offer, the fee depending mainly on how many megabytes of data files the host allows you to hold on the site. The smallest size is usually sufficient to start with. You can usually upgrade to a larger site later on.

If you look in a computer magazine, you will find advertisments for a dozen or more hosting services. The cost varies a lot between servers, depending partly on the size of storage supplied, and also on other facilities such as phone numbers for back-up technical advice. The cheaper companies may have slower download times, and some may spend an undue length of time off-line because of technical faults. But that is something you only get to know about after you have signed up.

Another copious source of hosting addresses is the Web itself. Use a search engine such as *Yahoo!* or *Google* and enter 'hosting' as the search word. You will obtain hundreds of addresses of servers offering to host your site. It is difficult to know which to choose, but there are sites that review the most popular servers and analyse their good points and their bad ones.

You will also need to settle on a domain name for your site. If the site is one of the cheaper ones, hosting 'family' web pages, you may be allocated a name automatically and free of charge. Typically this will comprise the name of the host, and your own name. For instance the format might be:

```
http://www.servername.com/yourname
```

This is fine if the only people to access your site will be family or friends. If you are building a commercial site and want a name that reflects the title of your business or describes its activities then you will need to choose a more descriptive name. You will also need to register the name so that there is no chance of anyone else having a site with the same name.

Domain name

To find an organisation to register your name, look in the computer magazines, or search the web, using 'domain' as the search word. Registration can be done on-line. Before you contact the register, prepare a short list of names that you would consider for your site. Before accepting the name you suggest, the register will search the Web to check that the name is not already taken.

You may need to submit several names before you hit on one that is available. Checking and registering a domain name usually incurs a fee, which you can pay on-line. Some organisations have special offers of free registration, but you might then find that you have to include advertising matter on your pages.

Transferring files

When you have been allocated a domain name, or have found an available name, you pay the required fees (if any). Then you are ready to put files on the area of the server's memory bank that they have set aside for your use.

The server will provide you with a password that allows you access to the site. You may also be offered file transfer software (free or at a reasonable cost). Some servers also provide software for developing web pages. These may or may not cater for placing applets on the site. In this book, we are assuming that you will be writing your own *HTML* pages directly, using *Notepad* or a similar simple text editor.

If the server does not provide the file transfer software, you will need to obtain it elsewhere. You need an FTP program. FTP stands for 'file transfer protocol' and is the standard technique for transferring files from one computer to another. There are several FTP programs available. You may sometimes find a simple one on the free cover disc of a computer magazine.

A very well-known FTP program is *WS_FTP Home*, published by Ipswitch. The software and the licence to use it is obtainable from:

www.ipswitch.com

This is the software we used for operating the website that we used for testing all the applets in this book. Full details for installing and using *WS_FTP Home* come with the download. The basic principle of the program is very simple.

Ipswitch also publish more advanced professional FTP software.

The FTP software operates with two folders. On the one hand is the folder you have set up on your computer's hard disc (drive C). On our computer this is called *WEBSITE*, but you can choose almost any name you like. *WEBSITE* contains the files that we want to transfer to the website. It also contains the program file for *WS_FTP Home* and associated files.

On the other hand, is the folder on the server's computer. Ours we have named *Applets*. This contains a number of files put there by the server and will soon contain the files for the website display.

The screen in *WS_FTP Home* is divided into two windows, left and right. The left window displays a list of all the files in *WEBSITE*. When the computer is connected to the website, the right window contains a list of all the files in *Applets*.

Between the two windows is a pair of buttons, one bearing an arrow pointing from left to right. The other button bears an arrow pointing from right to left. To transfer a file from WEBSITE to Applets or from Applets to WEBSITE, just select the file and click on the appropriate button. What could be simpler?

Website files

The one essential file is the *HTML* file that describes the page that opens when the site is first visited. By convention, this file is called *index.html* or sometimes *home.html*. It is the home page of the site.

The home page file may be sufficient on its own. However, if it contains photos or drawings, we must upload their files to the server. It may have links to other HTML pages, in which case the files of these pages must be included on the server's side. If these pages include images, or audio clips, their files must be there too.

In the same way, if the home page or any other page calls on applets, the *Java .class* files for these must be uploaded to the website, ready for use. A complicated website may depend on there being a hundred or more files stored on the server's computer.

The first applet goes on-line

Our website was set up as a test-bed for the applets in this book. We thought that we should include an explanation of this on the home page. This is for the benefit of any person who happens to visit the site and wonders what it is all about. Here is the listing of the HTML *index* file:

```
<HTML>
<HEAD>
<TITLE>The Applet Site</TITLE>
</HEAD>
<BODY BGCOLOR="#CCCCFF">
<H1><FONT FACE="Franklin Gothic Book"
COLOR="#FF0033"><CENTER><I>The Applet Site</I>
</FONT></H1>

<P><FONT FACE="Comic Sans MS" COLOR="#336633">This
is a site for testing <I>Java</I> applets before
publication in the new book,
<BR><I>Getting Started with Java Applets</I>,
<BR>to be published in 2006 by Bernard Babani Press
Ltd.</FONT></P>
</CENTER>
<BR>
<BR>
<P>Here is the sample applet:</P>
<BR>
<APPLET CODE="text.class" WIDTH="250" HEIGHT="150">
</APPLET>
</BODY>
</HTML>
```

We will not explain the details of the coding here, though most of the tags have pretty obvious functions. This file is given the name *index.html* and saved in the *WEBSITE* folder. From there it is transferred to the website, using *WS_FTP Home*.

Instead of using this, you could use the *LookAtThis.html* file (p. 11), but rename it *index.html*. Modify it slightly by including the extension .class in the APPLET tag, and add double quotes around the filename and the dimensions, as in the listing above.

Copy the text.class file into the WEBSITE folder and then transfer it to your website.

You are now ready to visit your website. Run *IE* (or other browser). Key in the address of your website.

If you have security software, such as *Norton Internet Security,* running on your computer, you may receive a warning at this stage. It asks if you are willing to allow applets to be loaded. Select 'Allow applets'.

Now you will see the home page of your site, complete with applet. Our original home page with its applet looked like this:

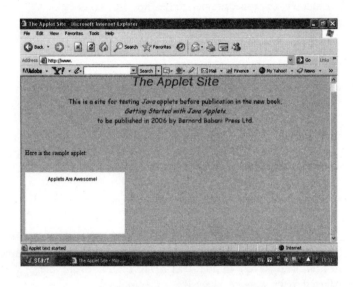

Fig. 6. Our test-bed site displays its first applet.

If you are using the HTML page listed on p. 11, the display will look like Fig. 2, p.13.

24

Browsers and other problems

If the screen does *not* look like Fig. 2 or Fig. 6, there are several possible reasons:

- You are not connected to your server. Check that your modem is switched on and has had time to connect you to the server.
- The website is not correctly set up. Check that you have followed the procedure detailed in the instructions from your server.
- You have mis-typed your password.
- There are typing errors in the *HTML* file or the *.java* file. This is not likely because these will have been discovered during compiling.
- The file name in the APPLET CODE= statement is not exactly the same as that of the *.class* file.
- You are using a browser other than *Internet Explorer, Firefox or Netscape*.

Different browsers interpret *HTML* files and the *Java* language slightly differently. All of the programs in this book have been tested with *Firefox*, *IE*, and *Netscape Browser* and, during development, on the applet viewer.

If you are using any other browser and the applet does not operate properly, the simplest thing to do is to install *Firefox* or *IE* and use that.

Firefox is available as a free download from:

www.firefox.com

At the time of writing, we found this the easiest to use. It runs all our applets without problems and it has a good bookmarking routine to give quick access to the website we used for testing out applets.

IE is available as a free download from:

www.microsoft.com/ie

This is the most popular browser and runs the applets reliably.

The Java Plug-in

If you are using *IE*, another possible source of difficulty concerns *IE* itself. The early versions of *IE* were able to run all programs written in the earlier versions (1.0 and 1.1) of *Java*. However, while Sun continued to develop newer versions of *Java*, Microsoft stopped upgrading *IE* to cope with these new versions.

Many applet writers avoid the difficulty by limiting their applets to methods and classes belonging to *Java* 1.0 and 1.1. But this means they can not employ the many effective and powerful methods and classes of the later versions. On the other hand, the relative simplicity of *Java* 1 has some advantages. We discuss this further in Chapter 4.

The solution to running *Java 2* with IE and other browsers is the *Java Plug-in* software. This causes the browser to run the standard *Java 2 Runtime Environment* (*J2RE*) software instead of running its own built-in software. The *Plug-in* operates with most browsers, including *Firefox*, *IE* and *Netscape Browser*.

The *Plug-in* is usually installed on your computer without your needing to do anything about it. If you have already downloaded *Java* from the Sun website, as you will have done if you are using this book, you will already have the software. If for some reason you do not have the *Plug-in* already installed, what happens is that the first time your computer tries to download a *Java 2* applet, it contacts the Sun website and automatically downloads and installs the *Plug-in*. This takes only a few minutes. From then on, the *Plug-in* remains in your computer and is used as and when required, automatically.

HTML converter

Like *javac*, *AppletViewer* and other software, *HTML converter* is part of the Java Development Kit (JDK) package downloaded from Sun. This program converts your *HTML* file with an applet embedded into it into a file that has the same name but with special converted code for running the applet.

This gets over difficulties with using certain browsers other than *IE* or *Netscape*, and with applets embedded by tags other than <APPLET>.

To use the converter, it is best if the HTML file to be converted is in the same folder as the *htmlconverter* program (usually the bin directory). Note that the converter normally converts *all* the HTML files in the folder at one go. But it creates a new folder called *bin_BAK*, to which it copies the original unconverted files before doing the conversions.

The converter is easy to use. Go to the Command screen and type the pathway to the bin folder (or whatever other folder holds the JDK. At the prompt type:

```
htmlconverter
```

Press 'Enter'. When the converter runs, a window appears asking for details of the required conversion. Usually there is no need to alter the entries already there, but check them to make sure. You will see that it also converts files with extensions *.htm* and *.asp*. Check the destination of the backup (unconverted) files. The click on the 'Convert' button. Conversion takes only a second or so.

The converted HTML file can be used just like the unconverted version. The difference is that previously the browser managed with whatever software it has for running Java. Now it uses the Plug-in. The applet viewer works with converted files too.

More applets

As you develop more applets in the remainder of this book, and create some of your own, you will need to be able to display them. The easiest thing to do is to prepare a short HTML page for each new applet. To make this simpler we prepared a short file called *htmltemplate.html*. This consisted of the bare necessities of a file that calls an applet. You load this into your text editor and add the details of the applet file you want it to call.

Overleaf is the text of our template.

```
<HTML>
<HEAD>
<TITLE></TITLE>
</HEAD>

<BODY BGCOLOR = "blue" TEXT = "white">
<H1></H1>
<P>
<APPLET CODE=".class" WIDTH="250" HEIGHT="150">
</APPLET>

</BODY>
</HTML>
```

To use this template, add a short descriptive title to remind you what
the applet does. Between <H> and </H> add a title (could be the same
one) to appear as a heading on the page. Add the applet file name just
before the .class extension. This must be exactly the same name as the
original .java file.

Edit the width and height to the same values as used in the .java file. If
you prefer other colours for the page backgound and text (see p. 155),
alter them in the listing.

Another way of displaying your applets is to have a single HTML file,
an index page. You add the HTML file name of each new applet as
you produce it, to a list that accumulate on this index page. Each item
on the lists needs the file name and a brief summary of what it does.

As an example, here is part of a list of some of the applets we have yet
to look at:

```
<BR>
<P>Click on the titles for other examples:
<BR>
<P><A HREF="caterpillar.html">Creepy-crawly text</A>
<P><A HREF="colourswap.html">Label flashing in two
colours</A>
<P><A HREF="digest7.html">Sounds triggered by
clicking</A>
<P><A HREF="digest7A.html">Sounds triggered by
mouseEntered</A>
<P><A HREF="digest8.html">Interface buttons</A>
```

This list goes between the end of the <APPLET> code and the closing </BODY> tag.

The list appears on the screen as a list of brief descriptions of the applets. Clicking on any one of the descriptions takes the viewer to the corresponding applet.

Do not type this example in yet. Build up your list, item by item, as you investigate each new applet.

4 J1 or J2?

This is a question that you might consider before you start writing your own applets, or modifying the ones in this book. There are both J1 and J2 applets in this book. You can easily recognise which is which. In *Java 1* (which includes *Java 1.1*) applets the class declaration includes the words 'extends Applet'. In *Java 2* applets the declaration is 'extends JApplet'. Among the imported packages J2 applets always list javax.swing.

You will probably also notice that *Java 1* applets are shorter. There are several reasons for this. Inevitably, if a language is rich with methods that can carry out a wide range of complex actions, it must require more detailed (and therefore longer) instructions as to exactly what is to be done.

Below we contrast two listings, one for *Java 1* and the other for *Java 2*. Before looking at these we should remember that, from the point of view of the person who views the applet using a browser, the *Java 1* applets can usually be run without a hitch. The browser itself provides the necessary interpreting. There may be problems with *Java 2* applets unless the *Java* plug-in is installed, as described in the previous chapter. Of course, this situation may change as a result of new versions of the browser becoming available.

From the point of view of the beginner there are other things to consider. The two listings below will help to make this clear, since they both produce exactly the same behaviour and the same display on the screen.

The two versions are listed side-by-side overleaf to make the comparisons easy. The actions of this applet are described in detail i n Part 3 (pp. 176-8). Here we look at the differences between them.

As anticipated on p. 30, the *Java 1* version is shorter. The *Java 2* version needs two additional imports, one for using *Swing* methods and the other for the extra event-processing methods of *Java 2*.

The class declarations extend Applet or JApplet, as appropriate. In the *Java 2* version, we also need to include 'implements ActionListener'. This is because Java 1 has relatively basic responses to events and all are dealt with without special implementation. In *Java 2* we need to implement listener methods for each of the types of event that may be needed in the program. Here we are concerned only with processing the action of clicking on one of the buttons. In other programs we may also need to implement mouse events, keyboard events and several others.

The definitions of global variables are the same for each version, except that *Java 2* uses JButton instead of Button.

The statements in the init() method are mainly the same in both versions. The difference is that, in *Java 1*, there is no need to create a panel equivalent to the ContentPane of Java 2.

There is a significant difference in the methods of handling events. For the beginner, the single *Java 1* method, action() is easier to learn and use than the extensive range of methods provided in *Java 2*.

The first significant contrast with the *Java 1* method is that action() returns a boolean value. actionPerformed() does not return any value. This is why the last statement in the *Java 1* version is return true. We do not use this feature in this example, but *javac* will not compile the program if this statement is omitted.

31

```java
import java.awt.*;
import java.applet.*;

/*
<APPLET CODE=digest8B WIDTH=450 HEIGHT=200>
*/

public class digest8B extends Applet{

//Workbench for interface buttons (Java 1 version).

    String response;
    Button clickOnMe = new Button("Click on me");
    Button orMe = new Button("... or me ...");
    Button orPossiblyMe = new Button("or possibly
me");

public void init() {

    FlowLayout dexter = new
 FlowLayout(FlowLayout.RIGHT);
    setLayout(dexter);
    clickOnMe.setBackground(Color.blue);
    clickOnMe.setForeground(Color.yellow);
    add(clickOnMe);
    orMe.setBackground(Color.red);
    orMe.setForeground(Color.black);
    add(orMe);
    orPossiblyMe.setBackground(Color.yellow);
    orPossiblyMe.setForeground(Color.red);
    add(orPossiblyMe);
    setBackground(Color.cyan);
}

public boolean action(Event e, Object ob) {

    if (e.target == clickOnMe) {
    response = "Blue button";}
    if (e.target == orMe){
    response = "Red button";}
    if (e.target == orPossiblyMe) {
    response = "Yellow button";}
    repaint();
    return true;
    }

public void paint (Graphics g) {
    g.setColor(Color.darkGray);
    g.drawString(response, 20, 80);
}}
```

```java
import java.awt.*;
import java.awt.event.*;
import javax.swing.*;

/*
<APPLET CODE=digest8C WIDTH=450 HEIGHT=200>
*/

public class digest8C extends JApplet implements
ActionListener {

//Workbench for interface buttons (Java 2 version).

    String response;
    String lastResponse = "";
    JButton clickOnMe = new JButton("Click on me");
    JButton orMe = new JButton("... or me ...");
    JButton orPossiblyMe = new JButton("or possibly
me");

public void init() {
    Container control = getContentPane();
    FlowLayout dexter = new
 FlowLayout(FlowLayout.RIGHT);
    control.setLayout(dexter);
    setBackground(Color.cyan);
    clickOnMe.addActionListener(this);
    control.add(clickOnMe);
    orMe.addActionListener(this);
    control.add(orMe);
    orPossiblyMe.addActionListener(this);
    control.add(orPossiblyMe);
    setContentPane(control);

}

public void actionPerformed(ActionEvent e) {

    if (e.getActionCommand() == "Click on me") {
    response = "Blue button";}
    if (e.getActionCommand() == "... or me ...") {
    response = "Red button";}
    if (e.getActionCommand() =="or possibly me") {
    response = "Yellow button";}
    repaint();
    }

public void paint (Graphics g) {
    Graphics2D g2D = (Graphics2D)g;
    clickOnMe.setBackground(Color.blue);
    clickOnMe.setForeground(Color.yellow);
    orMe.setBackground(Color.red);
    orMe.setForeground(Color.black);
```

33

```
          orPossiblyMe.setBackground(Color.yellow);
          orPossiblyMe.setForeground(Color.red);

       g2D.setColor(Color.cyan);
       g2D.drawString(lastResponse, 20, 80);
       g2D.setColor(Color.darkGray);
       g2D.drawString(response, 20, 80);
       lastResponse = response;

   }}
```

As already mentioned, there is only one event-handling technique in *Java 1*, and we do not have to implement this in the class declaration. There is a limited set of methods for events involving the interface components. These include action() as used in this listing for an action generated by a component. There are also methods for dealing with key events, mouse events and changes in input focus.

In the *Java 1* action() method, the component initiating the event can be identified by using the built-in target variable which holds the identity of the component. Here we test for equality between this and the various buttons. Note that the buttons are referred to by their object names.

In the *Java 2* actionPerformed() method we use the getActionommand() method to identify the component. This is tested for equality with the *text label* of the button, not on its *name*.

The biggest difference occurs in the paint() method. In *Java 1*, the colours of the buttons have been set in init(). We need only set the colour for the message and then draw it. In *Java 2* we first cast the graphics screen into its Graphics2D version. Then we set the button colours. It seems necessary to set these colours here. Otherwise, the buttons fail to appear on the display.

A further complication is that, in *Java 1*, as we click on the buttons in turn, the screen is automatically cleared before the new response is displayed. This ensures that the display is legible. However, this does not happen in *Java 2*. Each successive response overprints the previous responses.

To prevent this we add three lines to `paint()`. The previous response, `lastResponse` is printed in background colour, clearing the area. Then the current reponse is printed in dark grey. Finally, the last response is made equal to the current response, ready to overprint it when a button is next clicked.

Summing up, *Java 2* has superior features, but may not be readily displayed by the user's browser. Also the listings are longer. For the beginner writing their own programs, it could be better to concentrate on *Java 1* at first, and adventure into *Java 2* as experience is acquired. There are programs for both versions of *Java* in this book. You can also convert many of the Java 2 listings to Java 1 — the last section of the *Java Digest* shows you how.

Deprecated APIs

When you compile a listing written in *Java 1*, you may often be sent a warning message to say that your listing includes a deprecated API. This is a method of early versions of *Java* that has since been replaced by a better method in subsequent versions of the language. It is usually safe to ignore such warnings.

5 Internet sources

There is a lot of practical help and advice for *Java* programmers on the Internet. All are catered for, from beginners to the most advanced professional programmers. As the first step into *Java* programming, most people visit the site of Sun Microsystems to download a version of the language and associated files, such as *appletviewer*. The URL is:

http://java.sun.com

This site is now known as the *Sun Developer Network* (*SDN*). It has extensive facilities, including:

- Downloads of software (free at the time of writing).

- A reference section that lists and explains all the hundreds of current APIs.

- Code samples.

- Technical articles and tips.

- User groups.

- Newsletter.

- Blogs.

The abbreviation 'API' is often used but hardly ever explained. It stands for 'Application programming interface'. In other words classes and methods.

Of special interest to beginners (and others?) the SDN carries Learning Tutorials and Question.

A large and instructive site of special interest to applet writers is the *Java Applet Rating Service*. Its URL is:

http://www.jars.com

This site lists and rates applets submitted to the site by applet writers from all over the World. The applets are rated on a star system from * to *****. They are classified by type, for example utilities, games, business and tools. This is where to look when you are in a hurry and believe that someone before you must have had and solved the same problem.

The JARS site is not restricted to *Java* applets. There are applets written in *JavaScript, Active X , C++*, and other languages.

The Java World Magazine site is slightly different from the above two sites, as might be expected from it name. Its URL is:

http://www.javaworld.com

Its format is that of a technical magazine. It has numerous technical articles on all aspects of Java programming. In particular, it has an extensive section dealing with Readers' Queries. If you have any programming problems, just e-mail them to the magazine. They may then be put on the site for visitors to read. With any luck some other visitor will have a solution to your problem or a comment to make. In due course this solution will appear on the magazine site.

Three more sites of interest are at:

http://www.javaboutique.com
http://www.javashareware.com
http://www.gamelan.com

These carry a range of articles and tips on applet programming. They also have listings of applets including utilities, business applets and games. The *Gamelan* site has several tutorial articles and useful links to related sites.

Browsing

After visiting the five sites described above, you may want to explore further. Run your favourite browser and search with the keyword 'applet'. We did just this, using *Yahoo!,* which found over 15 milliion sites in 0.12 seconds. Applets are certainly awesome!

Images

Images, either photographs or drawings are often needed to make an applet more interesting or attractive. Perhaps you can take a digital photo or draw the required image using graphic software. But maybe you can not find a suiable subject for the photograph or you lack drawing skills.

Fortunately, the web is a rich source of images of all kind and of all subject matter. One such website is:

http://www.clipart. com

This has almost unlimited numbers of images including photographs, buttons, icons, fonts and sound clips.

If you are unable to locate a suitable image at this site, try an image search with *Google.* Their vast collection is almost certain to include the image you need.

Sounds

Usually, applets need only short audio clips lasting for a couple of seconds or so. If you need a special effect or a pre-recorded message, capture the sound with a microphone. Use audio software to save it as a .wav file.

Another possible source is a CD of sound effects or a CD or tape recording. But remember to obey copyright laws.

A useful source of sound clips on the Internet is:

http://www.a1freesoundeffects.com

This site carries many sound effects classified under different categories. You can listen to these and then download any that suit your applet. Downloads are usually free. The site also lists CDs of collections of sound effects, available at reasonable prices.

6 Motion pictures

There are several ways to achieve the illusion of motion. One way is to bodily move an image around the screen by plotting it in a series of locations, each slightly displaced from its neighbours. At each step the image is blanked out and replaced by the next displaced image.

The *moveAuto* program is an example of this. An image of a car appears at the left of the screen, moves steadily across, and disappears at screen right (Fig. 7). This sequence is repeated indefinitely, but the car can be stopped by clicking on the "Brakes" button. The button has toggle action, so the car starts again when the button is clicked a second time.

This program moves an Image object. The image can be any .gif file or .jpg file provided that it is not so large that repainting the display makes the action too jerky.

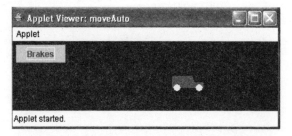

Fig. 7. The button at top left is used to start and stop the car.

40

```java
import java.awt.*;
import java.awt.geom.*;
import java.awt.event.*;
import javax.swing.*;


public class moveAuto extends JApplet implements ActionListener, Runnable
{
        Thread mover = null;
        int xDist = -20;
        Image car = null;
        JButton startStop;
        int inc = 3;

public void init() {

        Container road = getContentPane();
        FlowLayout arrange = new FlowLayout(FlowLayout.LEFT);
        road.setLayout(arrange);
        setBackground(Color.blue);
        startStop = new JButton("Brakes");
        car = getImage(getCodeBase(), "Auto1.gif");
        JPanel space = new JPanel();
        road.add(startStop);
        road.add(space);
        startStop.addActionListener(this);
        setContentPane(road);
}

public void start() {

        if (mover == null) {
                mover = new Thread(this);
                mover.start();
        }}

public void stop() {

        if (mover != null) mover = null;
                }

public void run() {

        while (mover != null) {
                xDist = xDist + inc;
                if (xDist >= 420) {
                xDist = 0;
                }
```

41

```
                        repaint();
                        try
                        {Thread.sleep(60);}
                                    catch(InterruptedException e){}
        }}

    public void actionPerformed(ActionEvent e) {
        if (e.getActionCommand() == "Brakes") {
                    if (inc == 3) {
                    inc = 0;}
                    else if (inc == 0) {
                    inc = 3;}
                    }
                    repaint();
        }

    public void paint(Graphics g) {
        startStop.setBackground(Color.green);
        startStop.setForeground(Color.darkGray);
        Graphics2D g2D = (Graphics2D)g;
        g2D.setColor(Color.blue);
        Rectangle2D.Float blankit =
    new Rectangle2D.Float(xDist - 5, 45F, 15F, 30F);
        g2D.fill(blankit);
        g2D.drawImage(car, xDist, 50, this);
    }}
```

The width of this applet is 400 and its height is 100. These parameters must be included in the HTML file or be embedded in this listing after the import declarations (see p. 18).

Operation

The program implements `ActionListener` to repond to clicking the button. It also implements `Runnable` and the thread `mover` controls the timing of the animation. The image is a simple outline of a car, drawn using graphics software (*Paint Shop Pro*). The image is 47×22 pixels and is stored in the same folder as the program file.

In `init()` we set up and add to a container, which is the usual procedure followed in this book for building the structure of an applet.

We use `FlowLayout` because the other types of layout need extra programming to obtain neat buttons, and we are trying to keep things simple. `JPanel` is used to create an area for the display.

Because there is a `thread`, we need to override the `start()` and `stop()` methods to take care of this.

The distance of the image from the left margin of the applet screen is the variable `xDist`. This is declared with a value -20, which puts the car just off the left margin. Every 60 ms, the `run()` method increments `xDist` by the amount `inc`, which is declared as 3. When `xDist` exceeds 420, the car is just off-screen, on the right. At this point, the `if()` method comes into action, reducing `xDist` to -20 again. So, as soon as the car has disappeared off the right side of the screen it reappears on the left.

The `run()` method simply waits for the Brakes button to be clicked and, if `inc` eqals 3, changes it to 0, which stops the car where it is. At the next click, `inc` currently equals 0 so `Run()` changes it to 3 and the car resumes its jouney.

The main action of the `paint()` method is to blank out the image of the car by drawing a rectangle, `blankit`, over it. This has the same colour as the background, so the car disappears. But before the eye has had time to register this fact, the car is redrawn in its new position, 3 pixels to the right. This gives the illusion of motion.

What next?

Moving things around the screen is a favourite way of attracting attention. If you can move a car, you can use a similar technique to move many other things — images of almost anything (including photo-images), single words of text or longer strings. You do not need to include the Brakes button, so you can omit that and the `actionPerformed()` method. Also delete the word `ActionListener` (and the comma) from the class declaration. Just let the thread run continuously.

Moving banner

If you have already typed in *moveAuto*, you can quickly edit it into this next program, *bouncer*. As you edit, tailor the display to produce the effect you want. Plenty of chances to be creative and, by experience, to become proficient at programming applets. Here is just one of many possible versions of *bouncer*. The width of this applet is 600 and its height is 200. These parameters must be included in the HTML file or be embedded in this listing after the import declarations (see p. 18).

Bouncer is a versatile program for displaying moving text.

```
import java.awt.*;
import java.awt.geom.*;
import java.awt.event.*;
import javax.swing.*;

public class bouncer extends JApplet implements
Runnable {

     Thread moverx = null;
     Thread movery = null;
     int xDist = 50;
     int yDist = 100;
     int incx = 2;
     int incy = 1;
     Font coolFont;

public void init() {

     Container road = getContentPane();
     setBackground(Color.blue);
     JPanel space = new JPanel();
     road.add(space);
     setContentPane(road);
     Font coolfont = new Font("Goudy Stout",
Font.PLAIN, 20);
     setFont(coolfont);
}

public void start() {

     if (moverx == null) {
             moverx = new Thread(this);
             moverx.start();}
     if (movery == null) {
             movery = new Thread(this);
             movery.start();}
```

44

```
public void stop() {
    if (moverx != null) moverx = null;
    if (movery != null) movery = null;
    }

public void run() {
    while (moverx == Thread.currentThread()) {
            if (xDist >= 380 || xDist <= 20) {
            incx = -incx;
            }
            try
            {Thread.sleep(40);}
            catch(InterruptedException e){}
            xDist = xDist + incx;
            repaint();
            }
    while (movery == Thread.currentThread()) {
            if (yDist >= 180 || yDist <= 20) {
            incy = -incy;
            }
            try
            {Thread.sleep(60);}
                    catch(InterruptedException e){}
            yDist = yDist + incy;
            repaint();
            }}

public void paint(Graphics g) {
    Graphics2D g2D = (Graphics2D)g;
    g2D.setColor(Color.blue);
    Rectangle2D.Float blankit =
 new Rectangle2D.Float(xDist - 40, yDist - 40, 260F,
50F);
    g2D.fill(blankit);
    g2D.setColor(Color.yellow);
    g2D.drawString("Java wins", xDist, yDist);
}}
```

The program moves a short text string within the applet window.
Motion is in both the x-direction (horizontal) and the y-direction
(vertical), 'bouncing' off the edges of the area when it reaches them.
For this, *bouncer* employs two threads, moverx and movery, to
generate motion in the two directions. The threads run independently.
Because the threads do similar things (though in different directions)
the run() method comprises two routines. These are identical except
for the values of the variables. This means, for example, that the string
may travel faster in one direction than in the other.

In other words, we duplicate the routines involving the threads, as can be seen also in the start() and stop() methods.

The init() method of this program is shorter than that of *moveAuto* because there is no button and no Action event.

Returning to the run() method, this has quite different logic. Instead of sending the moving object back to the beginning of its track when it reaches the end, this method controls the *direction* of motion. It does this, and achieves the 'bouncing' effect, by reversing the sign of incx or incy (as appropriate) whenever the string gets near the boundary of the JPanel. In the two conditional expressions, note the use of two unbroken vertical bar symbols to represent the logical OR operator.

When you have run the program, fine-tune it to produce the exact effect you want. The timing and speed depend on the values of incx and incy given when they are first delared. The area travelled depends on the minimum and maximum values allowed for xDist and yDist in the run() method. If you set up a different message, or change the font or its point size, you may need to alter the dimensions of the blankit rectangle.

This applet provides plenty of opportunity for creative programming. For instance, make the string change colour when it strikes a boundary. Or it could change font. It would be interesting for it to change font size gradually, to give the illusion of it approaching and receding from the viewer. This might mean adding a third thread.

Frame animation

This is the kind of animation used in the cinema or on TV. A series of still pictures is projected on to the screen, each slightly different from the one before it. If the pictures are projected in quick succession, we obtain the illusion of motion.

The minimum number of pictures required is two, projected alternately. However, the effect is better if we have more and in the next program we have four.

46

The subject of this sample animation is a brightly coloured coralfish swimming toward the left of the frame (Fig. 8). A shoal of smaller black fish is swimming in the opposite direction. Every so often (in fact, every four frames) the coralfish opens its mouth and one of the small fish swims in. At the same time the eyes of the coralfish roll down to inspect its capture.

The body of the coralfish stays in the same place with respect to the frame, but the small fish swimming from left to right make it look as if the coralfish is moving too.

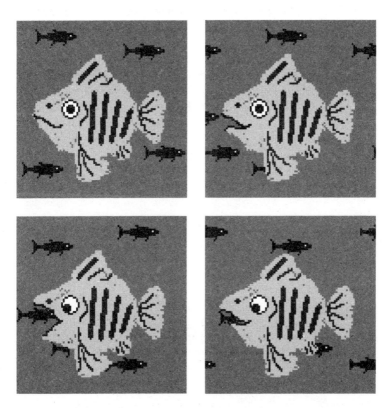

Fig. 8. The coral fish grabs its prey. The sequence runs from top left to bottom right, repeating.

The coralfish was drawn first, in yellow with bright blue stripes, using *Paint Shop Pro*. You could use other graphics software, but preferably one that lets you draw in pixels. The frame was small, 100 pixels square, to allow the image to be displayed quickly. But you could make yours a little larger, and it need not be square.

After drawing the first frame, saved as FISH01.gif, we re-loaded it and edited it to produce the second frame. The mouth starts to open and all the small fish are moved forward by one length. Where a fish is swimming out of frame to the right a 'new' fish appears at the same level on the left. Continue by editing/drawing the third and fourth frames. The fourth frame completes three-quarters of the action and the sequence repeats.

You need to have the program ready in order to see the result of your animation, so here is the listing. The width and height of this applet are 200. These parameters must be included in the HTML file or be embedded in this listing after the import declarations (see p. 18).

```
import java.awt.*;
import javax.swing.*;


public class coralfish extends JApplet implements Runnable {

        Thread swimmer = null;
        Image fish = null;
        String imageList[] = new String[5];
        int frame;

public void init() {

        Container ocean = getContentPane();
        setBackground(Color.lightGray);
        JPanel lagoon = new JPanel();
        ocean.add(lagoon);
        setContentPane(ocean);
        ocean.setVisible(true);
```

```
for (int j = 1; j < 5; j = j + 1) {
                imageList[j] = "FISH0" + j + ".gif";
                }
        }
public void start() {
        if (swimmer == null) {
                swimmer = new Thread(this);
                swimmer.start();
                }
        }
public void stop() {
        if (swimmer != null) swimmer = null;
        }
public void run() {
        while (swimmer == Thread.currentThread()) {

        repaint();
        frame = frame + 1;
        if (frame == 5) frame = 1;
        try
                {
                Thread.sleep(200);
                }
        catch(InterruptedException e) {}
        }}

public void paint(Graphics g) {

        Graphics2D g2D = (Graphics2D)g;
        fish = getImage(getCodeBase(), imageList[frame]);
        g2D.drawImage(fish, 50, 50, this);

}}
```

You can easily produce other 4-frame sequences to display, using this program. The most important thing to remember is to plan the cycle in equally-timed steps. Also, the fourth frame must lead smoothly back to the first frame.

If you like using graphics software (and like drawing!) design some longer sequences and adapt the program to animate them. You could even include short sound effects to be heard at suitable points in the cycle.

If you have a digital still camera capable of shooting short sequences, you could try to produce photo-animations. Software such as *Windows Media Player* (bundled with *Windows XP*) has editing facilities which allow you to pick out single frames from a video clip. Film a short repetitive action, then select a sequence of frames, and save them as still images. Then use them in a version of the *coralfish* program.

7 Tricks with text

Text that moves or changes its colour or font is a powerful eye-catcher. The main thing to remember is to keep it short. Otherwise it becomes an eye-teaser that it too difficult to read. This chapter explains ways of displaying text that attracts attention.

Typewriter

By using this technique we make a line of text appear on the screen character by character, in a way that resembles the action of an old-fashioned typewriter. The line of text is built up from left to right. When it is complete there is a pause of a few seconds, after which it is cleared and the cycle begins again.

On p. 52 is a listing of a short program that displays the message "Be yourself!!", in blue characters on a pink background. The characters are typed at the rate of 1 per 0.1 s, and there is a pause of 3 s before the complete message is cleared.

This program makes use of a `String()` method that we have not previously described. The substring() method selects a defined substring from a longer string. The method may have a single integer argument to specify the position of the character that is to begin the substring. The substring runs from that point to the end of the original string.

In this program, `substring()` has two integer arguments, specifying the beginning and end of the substring.

The width of this applet is 275and its height is 100. These parameters must be included in the HTML file or be embedded in this listing.

```java
import java.awt.*;
import java.awt.geom.*;
import javax.swing.*;


public class typewriter extends JApplet implements
Runnable {

    Thread typist = null;
    String text1;
    String segment;
    int count;
    int maximum;

public void init() {
    Container motto = getContentPane();
    setBackground(Color.pink);
    JPanel strip = new JPanel();
    motto.add(strip);
    setContentPane(motto);
    motto.setVisible(true);
    }

public void start() {
    if (typist == null) {
            typist = new Thread(this);
            typist.start();
    }}

public void stop() {
    if (typist != null) typist = null;
    }

public void run() {
    while (typist == Thread.currentThread()) {
            text1 = "Be yourself!!";
            maximum = text1.length() + 1;
            count = count + 1;

    try
    {
    Thread.sleep(100);
    }
    catch(InterruptedException e) {}
            if (count == maximum - 1) {
                    try
                    {
                    Thread.sleep(3000);
                    }
```

```
                catch(InterruptedException e) {}
                        }
                if (count == maximum) count = 0;

        repaint();
        }}

    public void paint(Graphics g) {
        Graphics2D g2D = (Graphics2D)g;
        g2D.setColor(Color.pink);
        Rectangle2D.Float tester = new
      Rectangle2D.Float(25F, 40F, 210F, 30F);
        g2D.fill(tester);
        g2D.setColor(Color.blue);
        segment = text1.substring(0, count);
        g2D.drawString(segment, 25, 50);
}}
```

The effect of typing is produced by a while ... loop that displays
a substring of gradually increasing length. The length increases from
zero when count = 0. The final length (maximum) is 1 greater
than the length of the original string. Remember that numbering of the
letters starts from zero. There is a delay of 0.1 ms in the loop to
simulate typical typing speed.

Each time round the loop, the display is cleared by overprinting it with
a rectangle, tester, of the same colour as the background. Then the
current substring is printed.

When the whole string has been displayed (count is 1 less than
maximum), there is a further delay of 3 s to allow the whole message
to be read. Then, on the next time through the loop, count is reset to
zero and the typing action is repeated.

More messages

The *typewriter* program is easily expanded to display a sequence of
messages. This version is called *typemottos*. Make the following
changes to the listing of *typewriter*:

1) Add these declarations to the global list at the beginning of the
program:

```
String[] texts;
int motto;
```

2) At the beginning of the `run()` method, insert this line to fill the `texts[]` array and select one of the messages:

```
        String texts[] = {"Too many cooks spoil
the broth.", Many hands make light work.",
"Absence makes the heart grow fonder.", Out of
sight, out of mind"};
        text1 = = texts[motto];
```

3) Delete the line:
```
        text1 = "Be yourself!!";
```

4) Expand the line beginning `if (count == maximum)` to this block:
```
        if (count == maximum) {
        count = 0;
        motto = motto + 1;
        if (motto == 4) motto = 0;
        }
```

The routine cycles through any number of text messages; if necessary, alter the '4' in the last line above to equal the number of messages to be displayed.

Text in a hurry

A different effect is produced by the *typescroll* routine. The message appears on the left, character by character. Then it travels across the screen and disappears on the right. The secret of this routine is that the message string has blank spaces added to it at either end.

As seen in Fig. 9, a string of 40 blanks is added at either end of the message. This allows room for a short message to scroll on to the screen and be read while passing. A longer blank string can be used for a longer message. The `substring()` method is used to select a 40-character string, for display.

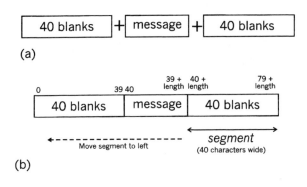

(a)

(b)

*Fig. 9. Scrolling a string: (a) two 40-blank strings are concate-
nated on to each end of the message, then (b) the substring () method is used to select a 40-character substring,
segment, the start of which is gradually shifted from right to
left. This makes the display scroll from left to right.*

Contrasting this routine with *typewriter*, in the previous program the
substring ran from zero in text1 to a position determined by the
value of the increasing count. In *typescroll*, the substring begins at
the value of the decreasing count and ends 40 characters later. Here
is the listing: The width of this applet is 275 and its height is 100.

```
import java.awt.*;
import java.awt.geom.*;
import javax.swing.*;

public class typescroll extends JApplet implements
Runnable {

    Thread typist = null;
    String text1 = "Be yourself!!";
    String pad = "                    ";  //20 spaces
    String padding;
    String padded;
    String segment;
    int count = 0;
```

```java
public void init() {
    Container motto = getContentPane();
    setBackground(Color.pink);
    JPanel strip = new JPanel();
    motto.add(strip);
    setContentPane(motto);
    motto.setVisible(true);
    }
public void start() {
    if (typist == null) {
            typist = new Thread(this);
            typist.start();
    }}
public void stop() {
    if (typist != null) typist = null;
    }
public void run() {
    while (typist == Thread.currentThread()) {
            padding = pad + pad;   // 40 spaces
            padded = padding + text1 + padding;   //
40 spaces both ends
            if (count == 0) count = text1.length() +
40;
    try
    {
    Thread.sleep(150);
    }
    catch(InterruptedException e) {}
    repaint();
    count = count - 1;
    }}

public void paint(Graphics g) {

    Graphics2D g2D = (Graphics2D)g;
    g2D.setColor(Color.pink);
    Rectangle2D.Float tester = new
 Rectangle2D.Float(10F, 30F, 180F, 25F);
    g2D.fill(tester);
    g2D.setColor(Color.blue);
    segment = padded.substring(count, count + 39);
    g2D.drawString(segment, 10, 50);
}}
```

The string of blanks could have been declared as a single string of 40 spaces but, for neatness, we decided to declare a 20-space string (pad) and double it by adding it to itself (padding). This is concatenated at both ends of text1 to produce padded. We then use substring() to select 40-character segments of padded.

Creepy-Crawly text

Text that acts like a live animal is guaranteed to attract attention. In this program, the word 'Caterpillar' (or a short phrase) creeps in undulating fashion across the screen from right to left. Given the principle, it is simple to devise other fascinating effects.

In any of the programs presented in this chapter it is possible to use different fonts and point sizes (see p. 158). This program looks and works best if the letters are of equal width. This is why we used the monospaced version of the default font. We set it at 16 points bold to make a distinctive display.

The program divides the original text into three sections, called `fore`, `hump` and `rear`. The `fore` section begins at the first character of the string (position 0), and continues to a position determined by `count`. The `hump` section contains only the next character. The `rear` section extends from the next character after `hump` to the end of the string.

The last three lines of the listing show that the three sections are drawn one behind the other, with the hump section a little higher on the screen than the other two sections. As the value of `count` increases from 0 to the full length of the text, the hump travels along the string from the fore end to the rear.

The distance of the 'caterpillar' from the left side of the screen is set by `xDist`, which begins with the value 170. This starts the caterpillar on the right. Each time the hump reaches the last character, the value of `xDist` is decremented, making the caterpillar advance toward the left.

Looking at the action in detail, the character of the hump is moved forward one space at the same time that it rises. This means that we need to know the width of a single space in pixels. The width depends on the typeface used and the point size of the characters. This requires a calculation. First, we generate a `FontMetrics` object that is based on the typeface being used. Call this `fm`. The expression `fm.stringWidth(text1)` returns the width of the *entire* string, in pixels.

The pixel width of a single character (space) is then found by dividing the string width by the number of characters, as returned by the expression text1.length(). The two quantities are both integers so it is possible that the division leaves a remainder, but this is ignored. However, this does not seem to introduce any problems. The width of this applet is 275 and its height is 100. The listing of *caterpillar* is:

```
import java.awt.*;
import java.awt.geom.*;
import javax.swing.*;

public class caterpillar extends JApplet implements
Runnable {

    Thread creepy = null;
    String text1;
    String segment;
    int count = 0;
    int xDist = 170;
    int space;
    String fore;
    String hump;
    String rear;

public void init() {
    Container crawly = getContentPane();
    setBackground(Color.pink);
    JPanel path = new JPanel();
    crawly.add(path);
    setContentPane(crawly);
    }

public void start() {
    if (creepy == null) {
            creepy = new Thread(this);
            creepy.start();
    }}

public void stop() {
    if (creepy != null) creepy = null;
    }

public void run() {
    while (creepy == Thread.currentThread()) {
            text1 = "Caterpillar";
```

```
            try
        {
        Thread.sleep(60);
        }
            catch(InterruptedException e) {}

        repaint();

                count = count + 1;
                if (count > text1.length()) {
                count = 0;
                xDist = xDist - space;
                    if (xDist < 20) xDist = 170;
                }
        }}

    public void paint(Graphics g) {

        Graphics2D g2D = (Graphics2D)g;
        g2D.setColor(Color.pink);
        Rectangle2D.Float tester = new
    Rectangle2D.Float(10F, 35F, 270F, 35F);
        g2D.fill(tester);
        g2D.setColor(Color.blue);
        Font face = new Font("Monospaced", Font.BOLD,
    16);
        g2D.setFont(face);
        fore = text1.substring(0, count + 1);
        hump = text1.substring(count + 1, count + 2);
        rear = text1.substring(count + 2,
    text1.length());
        FontMetrics fm = getFontMetrics(face);
        space = fm.stringWidth(text1) / text1.length();

        g2D.drawString(fore, xDist - space, 50);
        g2D.drawString(hump, xDist + space * count, 45);
        g2D.drawString(rear, xDist + space * (count +
    1), 50);

    }}
```

This program is another example of the usefulness of the
subString() method. It also introduces the FontMetrics class,
which enables us to find the dimensions of the typeface currently in use.
This information is important in cases such as this, where we need to be
able to plot the positions of strings with some precision.

Two other methods in this class are charWidth(), which returns the
pixel width of a given character and getHeight(), which returns the
height of the font in pixels.

Two-coloured text

A popular way to draw attention to a word or short phrase is to display it in two colours, alternately. *Colourswap* displays a phrase in red text for 1 s, then changes the colour to green, which it displays for a further 1 s. This repeats indefinitely. You can adapt the routine to any pair of colours and any timing.

The applet can be run as a stand-alone effect but it can also be displayed at the same time as other graphic or textual routines running in the same applet. Fig. 10 shows the *Netscape Browser* displaying the phrase "Believe it!" in red and green while the mottos of *typemotto* are being typed across the screen.

Fig. 10. Adding a second thread to the typemotto *applet makes it possible to flash the top line alternately in red and green.*

This applet illustrates how easy it is to program two independent actions to run simultaneously. We just set up two independent threads, one for each action.

To add the action to *typemotto*, first type in the *typemotto* listing (pp. 53-54). Then make the following amendments:

60

1) Change `typemotto` to `colourswap` in the <APPLET and class declaration lines.

2) Add these to the list of declarations:

```
Thread swapper = null;
boolean colourflag = true;
JLabel slogan;
```

3) In `init()`, after the line `motto.add(strip);` type in:

```
slogan = new JLabel("Believe it!");
strip.add(slogan);
```

We had previously added the `JPanel`, `strip`, to the `Container`, `motto`. Now we add the `JLabel`, `slogan`, to the `JPanel`. Flow layout is the default for a component such as this, so the `JLabel` should appear at top centre on the `JPanel`.

4) In `start()`, add a second conditional to make `swapper` start running:

```
if (swapper == null) swapper = new
Thread(this);
    swapper.start();
```

5) In `stop()`, add a second conditional to close `swapper`:

```
if (swapper != null) swapper = null;
```

6) The `run()` method requires an additional routine to alter the value of the `colourflag` flag variable from `true` to `false`, and `false` to `true`, alternately.

7) The result of alternating the value of `colourflag` is put into effect by these two lines in the `paint()` method:

```
if      (colourflag      ==      true)
slogan.setForeground(Color.green);
    else slogan.setForeground(Color.red);
```

Note that the background is white, as it can not be set for `JLabel()`.

Similar adaptations can be made to many of the programs in this book. It is easily possible to have three or more JLabels with different text, all flashing different colours at different rates. A spectacular experience!

8 Interactions

Moving pictures and fancy text displays are amusing to watch and add a lot to the effectiveness of a Web page. However, *Java* can do more than this — it can make the page interact with the viewer.

This chapter comprises a selection of short programs that illustrate some of the ways in which an applet can interact with the user.

Palette

The many colours of the text and graphics on a Web screen are the result of mixing red, green and blue in various proportions. *Java* has 13 predefined colours (p. 155), which cover most of our needs, but there are occasions when we would like to produce colours that are outside this range. As explained on p. 155, *Java* has a method by which the proportions of the three primary colours can be defined.

In practice, it is not easy to predict what a given proportion will look like on the screen. With this program you can try out any proportions you like and see the result straight away.

The applet has three `JTextField()` boxes, for red green and blue respectively (Fig. 11, opposite). Into each box we key a value between 0 and 255. As soon as we click on the boxes to confirm the entry, a large cirular area at the bottom of the screen displays the resulting colour.

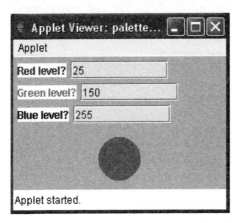

Fig. 11. The palette *applet displays a sky-blue disc, to show the result of mixing red, green and blue in the proportions 25:150:255.*

The listing is rather longer than usual because many of the commands have to be repeated three times, once for each colour. You can save typing time by first typing the short blocks of commands for red, then using Edit to copy the blocks and paste them twice, for green and blue. Finally, edit the pasted blocks changing 'red' to 'green' or to 'blue'. In a similar way, this description explains the programming for red, and it may be taken that the same applies to green and blue.

The listing (see over) begins in the usual way by importing needed packages, and declaring the *palette* class and the global variables. The program is primarily intended to demonstrate how to use the JTextField component.

The aim of the program is to accept input from a JTextField (redLevel) and eventually assign the entered value to the integer redLevel. Then redLevel is used as a parameter for defining the colour of the disc.

The init() method first declares a container pad, and sets this for flow layout. The two red components, a JLabel and a JTextField are set up and added to pad.

The width of this applet is 250 and its height is 150.

```java
import java.awt.*;
import java.awt.geom.*;
import java.awt.event.*;
import javax.swing.*;

public class palette extends JApplet implements
MouseListener {

JLabel redQuery;
JLabel greenQuery;
JLabel blueQuery;
JTextField redLevel;
JTextField greenLevel;
JTextField blueLevel;
String level;
int redValue = 0;
int greenValue = 0;
int blueValue = 0;

public void init() {

        Container pad = getContentPane();
        FlowLayout arrange = new
  FlowLayout(FlowLayout.LEFT);
        pad.setLayout(arrange);

        redQuery = new JLabel("Red level?");
        redLevel = new JTextField(10);
        pad.add(redQuery);
        pad.add(redLevel);
        redLevel.addMouseListener(this);

        greenQuery = new JLabel("Green level?");
        greenLevel = new JTextField(10);
        pad.add(greenQuery);
        pad.add(greenLevel);
        greenLevel.addMouseListener(this);

        blueQuery = new JLabel("Blue level?");
        blueLevel = new JTextField(10);
        pad.add(blueQuery);
        pad.add(blueLevel);
        blueLevel.addMouseListener(this);

        setContentPane(pad);
        setBackground(Color.lightGray);

}
```

```java
public void mouseClicked (MouseEvent e) {

        Object source = e.getSource();

        if (source == redLevel) {
                level = redLevel.getText();
                redValue = Integer.parseInt(level);
                }

        else if (source == greenLevel) {
                level = greenLevel.getText();
                greenValue = Integer.parseInt(level);
                }

        else if (source == blueLevel) {
                level = blueLevel.getText();
                blueValue = Integer.parseInt(level);
                }

        repaint();
        }

public void mousePressed (MouseEvent e) {}
public void mouseReleased (MouseEvent e) {}
public void mouseEntered (MouseEvent e) {}
public void mouseExited (MouseEvent e) {}

public void paint (Graphics g) {

        Graphics2D g2D = (Graphics2D)g;
        g2D.setColor(Color.lightGray);

        redQuery.setForeground(Color.red);
        greenQuery.setForeground(Color.green);
        blueQuery.setForeground(Color.blue);

        redLevel.setBackground(Color.yellow);
        redLevel.setForeground(Color.blue);

        greenLevel.setBackground(Color.yellow);
        greenLevel.setForeground(Color.blue);

        blueLevel.setBackground(Color.yellow);
        blueLevel.setForeground(Color.blue);

        Color blend = new Color(redValue, greenValue,
blueValue);
        g2D.setColor(blend);
        Ellipse2D.Float mixture = new El-
lipse2D.Float(100F, 90F, 50F, 50F);
        g2D.fill(mixture);
}}
```

A block of five lines sets up the red input side. It instantiates a new JLabel (redQuery), to label the new JTextField (redLevel). These two components are added to pad and then the JTextField is added to MouseListener.

The contents of pad are set and the background colour defined as light grey. Grey is used so that it does not produce a colour-cast on the coloured disc — a well-known optical illusion.

The mouseClicked() method is called every time the mouse is clicked on one of the text fields. The source is identified by the getSource() method. As a result, the string variable source holds the name of the text field.

A conditional statement ascertains if the source is redLevel. If so, the getText() method is used to assign the string value in the text field to the variable level. In the case of Fig. 11, for example, the value in level would be "25". But the Color() method called in paint() requires integer parameters. We use Integer.parseInt() to convert the string into the numerical value, 25, which is assigned to redLevel. The value typed in by the user has at last been assigned to the variable that holds the proportion of red that is to go into the final colour.

Before going on to the paint() method it is essential to key in the four unused MouseListener() methods with {} indicating 'do nothing' in each case.

The paint() method begins as usual by casting to Graphics2D. Then it sets the colours of the components. It is important to set a colour for the background of the text fields, otherwise they are not diplayed.

When repaint() is called at the end of the mouseClicked() method, the last four lines of paint() come into action. The new colour, (blend) is created by Color(), with an integer parameter for each of the primary colours. Then a circular ellipse is instantiated and filled with the blended colours.

Summing up (for red):

The required proportion of red in the new colour is typed as a text string into the text field redLevel.

When the mouse is clicked on redLevel, the string is temporarily stored in level.

It is immediately converted into an integer and stored in redValue. Then redValue is used in paint() as one of the integers that specify the new colour.

The colour is displayed as a disc.

Further developments

A likely source of error in using this program is to key in values that exceed 255. Write a routine to validate the input and reject it if it is out of range.

Essential Calculator

The *fourRules* program accepts two numbers A and B, and operates on them to display their sum, their difference, their product and their quotient. To perform a calculation you enter the two numbers in the text fields at the top of the screen. Then click on any one of four buttons labelled 'A + B', 'A - B', 'A*B' and 'A / B'.

The result of the operation is displayed immediately. Clicking on each button in turn, you can check the actions of the four basic rules of mathematics. Fig. 12 (overleaf) illustrates a typical calculation.

The listing has much the same structure as *palette*. It begins with declarations of global variables, which is followed by setting up the container, pad, and filling it with two labels, two text fields and four buttons. For simplicity we used flow layout and this happens to give a clear layout that is easy to use. This program implements ActionListener and the four buttons, sum, diff, product, and quotient, are added to this.

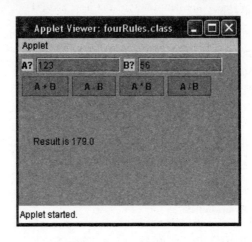

Fig. 12. The fourRules *program displays the result of adding 123 and 56.*

The main activity of this program takes place in the actionPerformed() method. It is called every time one of the buttons is clicked. First, we create an object, source, to hold the name of the button that was clicked. This will be "sum", "diff", "product" or "quotient".

Next, we read the values in the text fields by using getText(). These are strings, such as "123" and "56", but may also have decimal points, such as in "34.86". These strings are converted into floating point numerical values by Float.parseFloat() and assigned to AValue and BValue.

Finally, a set of conditional statements performs the selected mathematical operation on AValue and BValue to obtain the required result, ABValue.

The display is repainted to put this value on the screen.

The width of this applet is 300 and its height is 200.

```java
import java.awt.*;
import java.awt.geom.*;
import java.awt.event.*;
import javax.swing.*;

public class fourRules extends JApplet implements
ActionListener {

JLabel qtyA;
JLabel qtyB;
JTextField AQty;
JTextField BQty;
String Atext;
String Btext;
JButton sum = new JButton("A + B");
JButton diff = new JButton("A - B");
JButton product = new JButton("A * B");
JButton quotient = new JButton("A / B");
float AValue = 0;
float BValue = 0;
float ABValue = 0;

public void init() {

        Container pad = getContentPane();
        FlowLayout      arrange     =     new      FlowLay-
out(FlowLayout.LEFT);
        pad.setLayout(arrange);
        qtyA = new JLabel("A?");
        AQty = new JTextField(10);
        pad.add(qtyA);
        pad.add(AQty);
        qtyB = new JLabel("B?");
        BQty = new JTextField(10);
        pad.add(qtyB);
        pad.add(BQty);
        sum.addActionListener(this);
        diff.addActionListener(this);
        product.addActionListener(this);
        quotient.addActionListener(this);
        pad.add(sum);
        pad.add(diff);
        pad.add(product);
        pad.add(quotient);
        setContentPane(pad);
        setBackground(Color.orange);
}
```

69

```
        public void actionPerformed(ActionEvent e) {

        Object source = e.getSource();
        Atext = AQty.getText();
        AValue = Float.parseFloat(Atext);
        Btext = BQty.getText();
        BValue = Float.parseFloat(Btext);


        if (source == sum) ABValue = AValue + BValue;
        if (source == diff) ABValue = AValue - BValue;
        if (source == product) ABValue = AValue * BValue;
        if (source == quotient) ABValue = AValue / BValue;
        repaint();
}

 public void paint (Graphics g) {

        Graphics2D g2D = (Graphics2D)g;
                qtyA.setForeground(Color.blue);
                AQty.setBackground(Color.cyan);
                qtyB.setForeground(Color.blue);
                BQty.setBackground(Color.cyan);
                sum.setBackground(Color.cyan);
                sum.setForeground(Color.red);
                diff.setBackground(Color.cyan);
                diff.setForeground(Color.red);
                product.setBackground(Color.cyan);
                product.setForeground(Color.red);
                quotient.setBackground(Color.cyan);
                quotient.setForeground(Color.red);

                g2D.setColor(Color.orange);
                Rectangle2D.Float blankit = new
  Rectangle2D.Float(15F, 110F, 200F, 30F);
                g2D.fill(blankit);
                g2D.setColor(Color.blue);
                g2D.drawString("Result is " + ABValue, 20,
120);
 }}
```

The paint () method consists mainly of instructions for the colours of the components. These not only improve the appearance of the applet, but may also be essential when certain browsers are being used. The components may fail to appear or may disappear when other components are clicked on unless they are forced to stay on screen by setting their colours. Typing time can be reduced by copying and editing lines or blocks of text.

After setting the colours, paint generates an orange rectangle (the same colour as the background) to blank out the previous value of ABValue. The current value is then displayed.

Further developments

Java has a wide range of mathematical functions, so this program could be adapted to perform other calculations. These are included in the java.lang package and are accessed by calling 'Math' followed by the name of the function or a related keyword. For example, Math.sin() returns the sine of the argument. The argument is the size of the angle in radians. Similarly Math.max() returns the larger of the two arguments taken by this function. The arguments may be int, long, float, or double.

Here is a selection of maths functions:

Method	*Value returned*
abs()	Absolute value of the argument
acos()	Arc cosine of a radian angle
asin()	Arc sine of a radian angle
atan()	Arc tangent of a radian angle
atan2()	The angle that has the tangent x/y, where x and y are the two double arguments
cos()	Cosine of a radian angle
max()	Greater of two numblers
min()	Lesser of two numbers
pow()	First number to the power of the second number
random()	Random value between 0 and 0.999...
round()	Rounded to nearest integer
sin()	Sine of a radian angle
tan()	Tangent of a radian angle
toDegrees()	Turns degrees to radians
toRadians()	Turns radians to degrees

The Math package also includes two often-used mathematical constants, Math.PI and Math.E. The are both stored as doubles but can be cast into different numerical types by a command such as:

```
float P = (float)Math.PI;
```

P then holds the value of pi to 7 decimal places which is more than enough for most purposes.

Using these functions you could write a program to calculate the circumference of a circle given its radius and also calculate its area, and the volume and surface area of a sphere of the same radius. Another program could calculate increasing values of a capital sum at compound interest. An electronics enthusiast could find useful a program that calculates resistance, given voltage and current, or one that calculates the resonant frequency of a resistor-capacitor network.

Presentation

If calculating applets are to be useful, they should be easily accessible to be run as short programs. It is too much to have to call the Command line screen, navigate to 'bin'. and then type 'appletviewer ...'.

Instead, design an *HTML* page to hold the applet and explain how to use it. This can be listed among the favourite sites on your browser and so be instantly available. We have used bare-bones *HTML* pages while developing applets. An example appears on p. 11. Now look at this *HTML* listing of a slightly more elaborate page. It runs the fourRules applet.

```
<HTML>
<HEAD>
<TITLE>Calculator program</TITLE>
</HEAD>

<BODY BGCOLOR = "#FFCC00" TEXT = "blue">
<FONT FACE="Britannic Bold">
<H1>The four rules calculator</H1></FONT>
<FONT FACE="sans-serif">
```

```
<P>This program applies any one of the four basic
mathematical rules
 to two quantities, A and B.
<BR>
<P><FONT COLOR=teal>To use this program:
<BR>1) Enter the two numbers into the boxes below. The
numbers can
 have a decimal point, and may also be negative.
<BR>2) Click on one of the buttons.
<BR>3) The result appears just below the buttons.</FONT>

<CENTER>

<APPLET        CODE="fourRules.class"        WIDTH="300"
HEIGHT="150">
</APPLET>

</CENTER>

<FONT COLOR=Maroon>
<H2><I>You can repeat this as many times as you
like.</I></H2></FONT>
</BODY>
</HTML>
```

This is what it looks like:

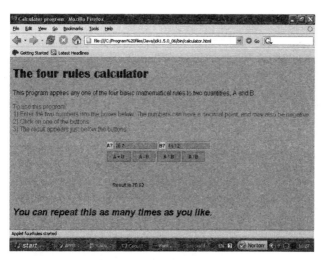

Fig. 13. The Calculator *page running off-line in* Firefox.

The *Calculator* program begins with the usual tags. Under <Body> we define the background colour as "#FFCC00', which gives a mixture of red and green that matches the orange colour of the applet background exactly. This merges the applet with the page.

The font for the main heading is *Britannic Bold*, but for the remainder of the page we adopt one of the built-in fonts, *sans serif*. This looks very much like *Arial*. Next comes the instruction text, displayed in teal, which is a dark blue-green.

Before inserting the *fourRules* applet we used the <CENTER> tag to place the applet in the centre of the screen. In the first trial run the height of the applet was specified as 200, the same value as in the applet listing. But this made the page too long to fit on the screen. To avoid the need to scroll the page, the height of the applet was reduced to 150 when calling the applet. Width and height specified in the *HTML* listing override the values specified in the applet.

Finally the centring is cancelled and the text colour is changed to maroon. The final text is displayed in the second-largest heading size and the <I> and </I> tags specify that the italic face is to be used.

The description above is intended to provide an illustration of how the *HTML* page can be made to look more interesting. It demonstrates how the applet format, compared with the format of the *Java* application, is such a convenient way of presenting a simple program. Instead of having to include everything in a *Java* application, the straightforward text, graphics and images can more easily be handled by the HTML page, leaving the 'fancy' effects to the applet. This applies on-line and off-line. It is an advantage of applets over and above their great importance in Web pages.

Keyboard input

A number of component methods are available for inputting data to a program. These include buttons, text fields, checkboxes and several other components. The mouse and keyboard are used for entering the data.

Usually the keyboard is used for typing in text and for entering numerical values. One further use for the keyboard, which does not seem to be commonly met, is the use of keys to directly control the action of a program. Games consoles have a joystick and we can use the keyboard as a substitute for this. The task is to implement this using the normal input components.

The listing below, *keyInput*, shows one way of getting the keyboard to provide input that can be analysed by logic statements and acted on accordingly. This is a 'bare bones' program that is simple to understand (see the note on p. 80). The width of this applet is 250 and its height is 150.

```
import java.awt.*;
import java.awt.event.*;
import java.awt.geom.*;
import javax.swing.*;


public class keyInput extends JApplet implements
KeyListener {

char key;
int letter;
JTextField register = new JTextField(0);


public void init() {
      Container base = getContentPane();
      FlowLayout arrange = new FlowLayout();
      base.setLayout(arrange);
      register.addKeyListener(this);
      base.add(register);
      setContentPane(base);
      setBackground(Color.lightGray);
}

public void keyTyped(KeyEvent e) {

      char key = e.getKeyChar();
      letter =(int)key;

      repaint();
}

public void keyPressed(KeyEvent e) {}
public void keyReleased(KeyEvent e) {}
```

```
public void paint(Graphics g) {

    Graphics2D g2D = (Graphics2D)g;

    g2D.setColor(Color.blue);
    g2D.drawString("Press any key", 20, 40);
    g2D.setColor(Color.lightGray);
    Rectangle2D.Float blankit = new
Rectangle2D.Float(15F, 50F, 120F, 30F);
    g2D.fill(blankit);
    g2D.setColor(Color.blue);

    if (letter == 97){
    g2D.drawString("Key pressed was 'a'.", 20, 60);
}}}
```

The width of the applet is 250 and the height is 150.

Fig. 14. The keyInput *demonstration program produces this display when the key pressed most recently is the letter 'a'. The program is case-sensitiv.e*

76

The task of this program is to accept typed input, though not neccesarily to display it. Instead it may trigger a wide range of other actions. We use one of the existing interface components to do this and have defined a text field called `register` to do this. Note that it is declared with a text length of zero and is added to `KeyListener`.

`KeyListener` has three methods, of which we use `keyTyped()`. The other two must be typed into the program with empty {} brackets. The `keyTyped()` method generates an event when a key is pressed. The identity of the key is found by using `getKeyChar()` This returns a char variable which we store in the previously declared char variable, `key`. In this form it is not so easily used in logical operations, so we cast the char variable into an int variable, called `letter`.

The value in `key`, and subsequently in `letter`, is a numerical value representing the Unicode for the character held there. This can take any value in the range 0 to 65536 but most of these are very specialised characters which do not appear on our Qwerty keyboard. We need to identify only the alphabetic and numeric symbols, and a few others that have codes 0 to 255. These, incidentally, are members of the ASCII code set and have the same values.

The lower-value Unicodes are:

- 0 to 31: control characters, such as 'carriage return', 'bell' (produces a beep in modern computers, but used to ring an actual bell in the old Teletype machines), and 'end of file'.

- 32: a space.

- 48 to 57: numerals 0 to 9.

- 65 to 90: capital letters A to Z.

- 97 to 122: lower-case letters a to z.

The codes in between these blocks are mainly punctuation marks. In the listing we are look for key 'a' to be pressed. This has the code 97. We use this value in the conditional statement in the `paint()` method, with the result that an 'a' is displayed when the 'a' key is pressed but nothing happens when other keys are pressed.

There is still a trace of the JTextField, which appears as a very narrow stripe at the top of the screen, but this will not be noticed when the screen is filled with brightly coloured fast-moving text and other images.

You can look up the ASCII code or Unicode in a reference book but a simpler way to discover the key codes is to type this line into the keyTyped() method of *keyInput*. enter it just before the repaint() command in the keyTyped(method:

```
System.out.println(letter);
```

Re-compile, then run the program in *Applet Viewer*. Have the command screen visible and watch for the values of letter to appear as you press different keys.

Moving disc

The *moveIt* program is an elementary illustration of how key input can be used. You can obtain this program by editing the *keyInput* file as follows:

1) Amend the class declaration to the new file name, moveIt.

2) Add an int variable called xDist to the list of global variables.

3) Amend the paint() method to the version shown opposite. Note that there are now only two closing brackets in the last line.

When the program is run, the "Press < or >" message appears. Just below it on the left is a red disc. Pressing the '>' key makes the disc glide to the right. This is done by the logic at the end of paint(), which increments xDist if the > key is pressed. Actually, as far as the program is concerned, we are operating in lower-case mode and it is the '.' that the logic is looking for. This has code 46. Conversely, pressing the < key gives code 44, the code for a comma, and the disc is moved from right to left. The logic does not allow xDist to be incremented or decremented if this would move the disc beyond the ends of its range, 21 to 199.

```
public void paint(Graphics g) {

       Graphics2D g2D = (Graphics2D)g;

       g2D.setColor(Color.blue);
       g2D.drawString("Press < or >", 20, 40);
       g2D.setColor(Color.lightGray);
       Rectangle2D.Float blankit = new
 Rectangle2D.Float(15F, 50F, 220F, 30F);
       g2D.fill(blankit);

       Ellipse2D.Float disc = new Ellipse2D.Float(xDist,
50F, 20F, 20F);
       g2D.setColor(Color.red);

       if (letter == 46 & xDist < 200) xDist = xDist +
1;
       if (letter == 44 & xDist > 20) xDist = xDist - 1;
       g2D.fill(disc);
}}
```

The width of this applet is 300 and the height is 200.

Using this program as a model, try giving the disc vertical mobility as well. Convenient keys to use are 'a' for up and 'z' for down. The code for 'z' is 122.

If a player presses a key other than '<' or '>', nothing will happen. This does not matter in this program but in some other programs pressing the wrong key may cause problems. Then we need a routine to check that the key pressed is allowable. The *validate* program on p. 101 demonstrates a way of checking key input.

Input and Output with files

The data held in an applet is lost when the applet is closed. It would be handy to be able to save the data on closing and to read it back the next time the applet is run. *Java* has methods for writing to files and for reading from files, but these methods will not work with applets. If you try to use the file methods with an applet, *Java* throws a SecurityException and will proceed no further with the program.

79

In one way, this is a disappointment. However, it illustrates the fact that applets do not have access to your files. We need not worry over security when an applet appears on the screen.

9 Codes and Ciphers

The terms 'code' and 'cipher' always seem to go together, like 'ham' and 'eggs' but, like ham and eggs, codes and ciphers are two entirely different things. Both codes and ciphers are systems for conveying information, often so as to keep it secret, but there the similarity ends.

With a **cipher**, we take a piece of text and replace each of its characters by a different one or alter the order of the characters in a systematic way. The process is called **enciphering**, or encryption (meaning 'to hide'). Enciphering makes it difficult for anyone to understand the text if they do not know how it was enciphered. It does not necessarily make it *impossible* to decipher the text. There are techniques for getting at the content of a cipher without knowing exactly how it was derived. The point is that deciphering takes time; by the time the cipher has been 'broken' by an unauthorised person it may be too late to make use of the information it contains.

A **code** ususally consists of a group or groups of characters. Each *group* has a predetermined meaning. For example in the Q code, for international telecommunications, the group QTC means 'How many telegrams do you have to send?'. The recipient of such a message has a **code book** in which they look up the code to discover the message. Without the code book, it is virtually impossible to understand the message.

Codes are often used for secrecy. Also they may be used because the codes are much shorter than the messages they convey. This saves time and money when communicating.

A code is not necessarily used for secrecy. Instead, it may be used for convenience. An example is the ASCII code, the *American Standard Code for Information Interchange*, which codes the letters of the alphabet, the numerals, punctuation marks, and certain instructions such as 'new line'. These are coded into seven-bit groups for transmission from one electronic terminal to another. The code replaces written or printed characters by sequences of binary signals. As with any other code, turning text into ASCII code and turning it back again requires a 'code book', in this case a computer program.

The computer programs themselves are written using code. The instructions stored in digital form in the memory of a computer tell the microprocessor exactly what to do at each stage of its operation. To produce this code, often known as *machine code* because it is 'understood' by the computer (the machine), the programmer uses a special type of software. The programmer writes this in *assembler code,* which is easier (for humans) to understand than machine code. The software then converts this code to its machine code equivalent.

In this chapter we describe some programs based on well-known code and cipher techniques. In each case our starting point is a piece of ordinary text, known in the world of codes and ciphers as **plain text**. As might be expected, the programs in this chapter present numerous examples of the *Java* methods for handling strings.

A simple enciphering program

This is perhaps the simplest of all enciphering techniques, known to every schoolchild. However, this program enciphers the text faster than can be done with pencil and paper — and it makes no mistakes.

The principle is simple substitution. We write out the letters of the alphabet in a row and, in a row below, write out a second alphabet, but shifted a number of places to the left, in the example below by three characters:

```
a b c d e f g h i j k l m n o p q r s t u v w x y z
d e f g h i j k l m n o p q r s t u v w x y z a b c
```

To encipher a message, we first write it out as plain text. Then, for each letter of the text, we look in the upper row of letters, and beneath it, write the corresponding letter from the bottom row. This is the cipher. For example, shifting by three places:

Plain text: T h i s i s t h e m e s s a g e
Cipher: w k l v l v w k h p h v v d j h

Word length provides a clue to the decipherer so we will make things more difficult by using 'z' instead of a space in the plain text. In cipher this becomes 'c'. The cipher now looks like this:

w k l v c l v c w k h c p h v v d j h

Fig. 15 shows the program in action.

Fig. 15. Type the plain text into the top window and the amount of shift in the small window below. Click on the 'Encipher' button and the cipher appear in the lower window.

The listing runs from here to p. 86.

```
import java.awt.*;
import javax.swing.*;
import java.awt.event.*;


public class cipher1 extends JApplet implements
ActionListener, Runnable {

Thread cipherit = null;
String word;
int wordLength;
int posn;
JTextArea plainText;
JTextField offset;
JButton encipher;
JTextArea cipherText;
String cipher = "";
boolean enFlag;
String letter;
String alphaLetter;
String cipherLetter;
String alpha;
String alphax2;

public void init() {

    Container base = getContentPane();
    FlowLayout arrange = new FlowLayout();
    base.setLayout(arrange);
    plainText = new JTextArea(4, 25);
    offset = new JTextField(5);
    base.add(plainText);
    base.add(offset);
    encipher = new JButton("Encipher") ;
    encipher.addActionListener(this);
    base.add(encipher);
    cipherText = new JTextArea(4, 25);
    cipherText.setEditable(false);
    base.add(cipherText);
    setContentPane(base);
    setBackground(Color.cyan);

    alpha = "abcdefghijklmnopqrstuvwxyz";
    alphax2 = alpha + alpha;
}

public void actionPerformed(ActionEvent e) {
    enFlag = false;
```

```
if (e.getActionCommand() == "Encipher") enFlag =
true;
    repaint();
}

public void start() {

    if (cipherit == null) {
    cipherit = new Thread(this);
    cipherit.start();
    }
}

public void stop() {

    if (cipherit != null) cipherit = null;
}

public void run() {

    while (cipherit == Thread.currentThread() ) {
    if (enFlag == true) {
            String word = plainText.getText();
            word = word.toLowerCase();
            int wordLength = word.length();
            word = word.replace(' ', 'z');
            int distance =
 Integer.parseInt(offset.getText());

            for (int j = 0; j < wordLength; j = j +
1) {
                    letter = (word.substring(j,
j+1));
                    for (int k = 0; k < 26; k = k+1)
{
                            alphaLetter =
(alpha.substring(k, k+1));
                            if
(letter.equals(alphaLetter)){
                                    posn = k +
distance;
                                    cipherLetter =
(alphax2.substring(posn, posn + 1));
                                    break;
                            }
                    }
                    cipher = cipher + cipherLetter;
            }
            cipherText.setText(cipher);
            enFlag = false;
    }
    repaint();
    }
}
```

```
public void paint(Graphics g) {
    Graphics2D g2D = (Graphics2D)g;
    plainText.setBackground(Color.lightGray);
    plainText.setForeground(Color.blue);
    offset.setBackground(Color.lightGray);
    offset.setForeground(Color.blue);
    encipher.setBackground(Color.red);
    cipherText.setBackground(Color.lightGray);
    cipherText.setForeground(Color.blue);

}}
```

The width of the applet is 300 and the height is 250.

The init() method follows the frequently used pattern, and the container is filled, in this order, with a text area plainText to receive input, a text field offset to receive the number of characters for the left shift, a button Encipher to start enciphering and a second text area cipherText to diplay the cipher.

Init() also declares to string variables, alpha, which is a list of the letters of the alphabet, and alphax2 which lists the alphabet twice.

The actionPerformed() method shows how to make the program wait for the plain text and shift value to be keyed in before going on to the enciphering routine. This technique has many applications in other programs. It relies on a boolean variable enFlag. The method resets this to false. It stays false indefinitely, but is changed to true when an event occurs.

Of the components in the container, the only one that matters is the encipher button. When this is clicked on, it generates an event and the method identifies this as coming from the button.This results in enFlag being changed to true. More later.

The main action of the program occurs in the run() method. This is a short routine. As in many *Java* programs, most of the program lines are concerned with declaring variables and painting the display.

As usual, the run() method is completely enclosed in a while...
loop, which keeps the method operating for as long as the thread is
active. Immediately inside this is an if... loop, which contains all the
enciphering routine. In this way, the enciphering routine is by-passed
until the encipher button is clicked and enFlag becomes true.

The first steps in the routine prepare the plain text for enciphering.
They also illustrate some useful string handling methods:

plainText.getText() fetches the text that has been typed into
the plainText text area. It is assigned to the string variable word.

word.toLowerCase() changes all uppercase characters to lower
case. This helps to make deciphering more difficult.

word.length() returns an integer wordLength equal to the
number of characters in the plain text (including spaces).

word.replace(' ', 'z') replaces every space in the text with a
'z'. This helps to hide the lengths of individual words.

offset.getText() fetches the text that has been typed into the
offset text field. This is a string of numerical characters. To
convert it to an integer, distance, we use
Integer.parseInt().

The kernel of the routine is a set of nested loops and conditional
statements. The outer loop is a for... loop with loop variable j. This
selects each character in the plain text from left to right. For every value
of j, the substring() method picks out a single-character string,
letter, which is the jth character in the plain text.

Given letter, the inner for ... loop (loop variable k) searches
the alphabet (string alpha) assigning each letter in turn to
alphaLetter. It matches this against letter and, if they are equal,
it knows that letter is the kth letter of the alphabet.

In the conditional expression in the inner loop we do *not* use if
(letter == alphaLetter). They can not be equal because they
are objects orginated in different ways. But they are the same letter and
the conditional expression uses the equals() method, which returns
a boolean value.

The next step is to calculate the position in `alphax2` of the enciphered equivalent letter, `cipherLetter`. The position is found by adding k to the previouly determined offset value, `distance` and using the result in `substring()`.

This routine illustrates the use of the keyword `break`, which appears in the inner loop. Having found a match, there is no point in the routine running on to examine the remainder of the alphabet for further matches. There are only two letters in `alphax2` that match the *k*th letter of `alpha` and its first occurrence has been found. This is all that is needed. The keyword `break` appears just after the line in which a value has been assigned to `cipherLetter`. It causes the processor to jump out of the inner `for...` loop and go to the next line in the outer loop. Here the current `cipherLetter` is added to `cipher`, gradually building up the enciphered text.

When all the letters in the plain text have been enciphered, the outer loop ends and the enciphered text is displayed in the lower text area, using the `setText()` method. Then, `enFlag` is reset to false, so the routine is not repeated unless the button is clicked on again, when it produces the same result.

Things to do

There are several ways in which *cipher1* could be improved. Try to program some of the improvements:

1) Improve the display by labelling the text areas and text field using `JLabel()`. Labels could be: 'Type plain text here', 'Amount of shift?', and 'This is the enciphered text'.

2) Write a routine to check that no numeric characters or punctuation are accepted when keying in the plain text.

3) Write a routine to check that the shift is keyed in numeric characters and has a value in the range 0 to 25.

4) To make deciphering more difficult, ciphers are often broken into groups of five characters. For example, the cipher on p. 83 becomes:

wklvc lvcwk hcphv vdjha

An 'x' has been added at the end to make the final group up to five characters. When enciphered with a shift of four, this becomes 'a'.

Deciphering

Formerly, the cryptologist had to employ laborious methods to find the message hidden in a ciphered text. The methds included finding the most frequently-occurring letters, and looking for repetitions of given groups of letters. Gradually the message was unravelled and the plain text revealed.

Nowadays, computers can be used for deciphering, and 'brute force' techniques can be used that were not practicable in the old days. The *cipherBreaker* program (p. 91) is an example of this. But first we will look at a program to save you the tedious work of deciphering — provided that you know the amount of shift.

If you have keyed in *cipher1*, you can quickly edit it to operate in the reverse direction. We will simply list the changes to be made:

1) Change the file name to `decipher1`, in the class definition.

2) Change the thread name to `decipherit`, throughout the program.

3) Change `plainText` to `cipherText` throughout.

4) Change `cipherText` to `plainText` throughout.

5) Change the name of the button and the text on the button to `decipher`, throughout.

6) Change the namc of the boolean flag to `enFlag` throughout.) Declare the global variable: `String text = "";`

7) Declare the global variable: `int shift;`

8) There are several changes in the `run()` method. The complete listing for this is shown overleaf.

```
public void run() {
    while (decipherit == Thread.currentThread() ) {

    if (deFlag == true) {
            String word = cipherText.getText();
            word = word.toLowerCase();
            int wordLength = word.length();
            int distance =
Integer.parseInt(offset.getText());

    for (int j = 0; j < wordLength; j = j + 1) {
            cipherLetter = (word.substring(j, j+1));
            for (int k = 0; k < 26; k = k+1) {
            alphaLetter = (alpha.substring(k, k+1));
            if (cipherLetter.equals(alphaLetter)){
                    posn = k - distance + 26;
                    letter =
(alphax2.substring(posn, posn + 1));
                    break;
                    }
            }
                    text = text + letter;
                    text = text.replace('z', ' ');
            }
            plainText.setText(text);
            deFlag = false;
    }
    repaint();
    }
}
```

The width is 300 and the height is 200.

Most of the changes above are simply changes of name to reflect the
fact that this program works from cipher back to plain text. The cipher
is typed into the top text area, and the known shift typed into the small
text field. The decipher button is pressed and the plain text appears in
the lower text area.

The run() method operates in a similar way to that in the *cipher1*
program but many of the operations are reversed. One difference is
that, when calculating posn, (the position of the alphaLetter in
alphax2, we add 26 to it. This takes us to the *same letter* but in the
second alphabetical run in alphax2. It allows distances of up to 25
to be subtracted from k without making posn negative.

Again we use break to halt the search as soon as a match has been found.

If we do not know how far the alphabet has been shifted during ciphering, the only thing to do to decipher the text is to try all possible values of shift until we get an intelligible message. Working with pencil and paper this can be a tedious job. But a computer can do it in a flash. This is one of the reasons that the invention of computers has had such an influence on cryptography.

When using the next program, which is the 'brute force' deciphering program mentioned earlier, the cipher is typed into the upper text area, but nothing is typed into the small text field. We simply click on the decipher button. The value '1' appears in the text field and text appears in the bottom rectangle. This is the cipher shifted back one position. This may or may not be a readable message. If it is, deciphering is complete. If it is not, click on the button again to see what two shifts will do. In short, continue clicking until you see the deciphered text.

Basically, this is the *decipher1* program set in a loop that increments distance from 0 upwards instead of reading it from the text field. An important difference is that the result is displayed by using drawString(), instead of a text field. This makes the listing of cipherBreaker1 different at several points. It can still be obtained quickly by editing but, to avoid confusion, the complete listing is as follows.

```
import java.awt.*;
import javax.swing.*;
import java.awt.event.*;
import java.awt.geom.*;


public class cipherBreaker1 extends JApplet
implements ActionListener, Runnable {

Thread decipherit = null;
```

```
        String word;
        int wordLength;
        int shift;
        int posn;
        JTextArea plainText;
        JTextField offset;
        JButton decipher;
        JTextArea cipherText;
        String text = "";
        boolean deFlag;
        String letter;
        String alphaLetter;
        String cipherLetter;
        String alpha;
        String alphax2;
        int distance = 0;

        public void init() {
            Container base = getContentPane();
            FlowLayout arrange = new FlowLayout();
            base.setLayout(arrange);
            cipherText = new JTextArea(4, 25);
            offset = new JTextField(5);
            base.add(cipherText);
            base.add(offset);
            decipher = new JButton("Decipher") ;
            decipher.addActionListener(this);
            base.add(decipher);
            setContentPane(base);
            setBackground(Color.cyan);

            alpha = "abcdefghijklmnopqrstuvwxyz";
            alphax2 = alpha + alpha;
        }

        public void actionPerformed(ActionEvent e) {
            deFlag = false;
        if (e.getActionCommand()  ==  "Decipher")  deFlag  =
        true;
            repaint();
        }
        public void start() {
            if (decipherit == null) {
            decipherit = new Thread(this);
            decipherit.start();
            }
        }

        public void stop() {
            if (decipherit != null) decipherit = null;
        }
```

```
public void run() {

while (decipherit == Thread.currentThread() ) {

    if (deFlag == true) {
            text = "";
            String word = cipherText.getText();
            word = word.toLowerCase();
            int wordLength = word.length();
            distance = distance + 1;
            if (distance == 25) distance = 1;

    for (int j = 0; j < wordLength; j = j + 1) {

            cipherLetter = (word.substring(j, j+1));
            for (int k = 0; k < 26; k = k+1) {
            alphaLetter = (alpha.substring(k, k+1));
            if (cipherLetter.equals(alphaLetter)){
                    posn = k - distance + 26;
                    letter = (alphax2.substring(posn,
posn + 1));

                    break;
                    }
            }
            text = text + letter;
            text = text.replace('z', ' ');
    }
    String shift = Integer.toString(distance);
            offset.setText(shift);
            deFlag = false;
            repaint();
    }}
}

public void paint(Graphics g) {
    Graphics2D g2D = (Graphics2D)g;
    offset.setBackground(Color.lightGray);
    offset.setForeground(Color.blue);
    decipher.setBackground(Color.red);
    cipherText.setBackground(Color.lightGray);
    cipherText.setForeground(Color.blue);

    g2D.setColor(Color.lightGray);
    Rectangle2D.Float blankit = new
 Rectangle2D.Float(10F, 110F, 280F, 110F);
    g2D.fill(blankit);
    g2D.setColor(Color.blue);
    g2D.drawString(text, 12, 120);

}}
```

The width of this applet is 300 and the height is 200. In the two previous programs, we had to read the shift value, in the offset text field (which was a string) and convert it into an integer, distance. In *cipherBreaker1,* we need the inverse conversion from integer to string. This is so that the current value of distance can be displayed in the text field.

The conversion is performed by another of the many methods for strings, Integer.toString(). The string shift is then displayed in the text field by using the method setText().

Something to try

It is fairly easy to break this simple substitution cipher, even if we do not know the amount of shift. This is because the letters of the alphabet are in the standard order, making calculations simple. It is much more difficult to break the cipher if the letters are not in order.

One way of ordering the letters differently is to use a **password**. The letters for the plain text are in normal alphabetical order but when we write the cipher letters beneath them we begin by writing the password, followed by the remainder of the alphabet. Suppose the password is 'computing'. The two alphabets are set out like this:

```
a b c d e f g h i j k l m n o p q r s t u v w x y z
c o m p u t i n g a b d e f h j k l q r s v w x y z
```

Now there is no way of deciphering by a simple mathematical routine. You have to know the password. Note that the password must not have two letters the same.

Try writing a program which first asks the user to key in a password, and then sets up the two alphabetical strings required for enciphering. This program does not need to be given a shift value. Then it works through the message, finding its letters in the top row and replacing them with the corresponding letters from the bottom row. You will also need a deciphering program, which is told the password and then performs the inverse operation.

Transposition ciphers

Another group of ciphers works not by substituting one letter with a different letter, but by keeping the same letters and mixing them into a different order. This has to be done in a systematic way so that the message can be deciphered by the reverse operation.

Many transposition systems have been invented and one of the easiest to understand (and program) is known as **geometric transposition.** The message to be enciphered it written in an array or matrix which has a definite geometrical form. We will base the program, *cipher2,* on the most obvious of geometrical forms, the rectangle. However, many other forms as possible, limited only by the imagination of the cryptographer.

A rectangle has the form of a two-dimensional array. However, although *Java* is rich in methods for processing arrays, there is no need for arrays in this program. For this example, we set out the letters of the message in a rectangular array (but not an array in the *Java* sense) that has three columns and as many rows as are needed to contain the message. Supposing that the message is:

Meet at the clubhouse tonight

This is written out, all in lower case and omitting spaces and punctuation:

```
m e e
t a t
t h e
c l u
b h o
u s e
t o n
i g h
t
```

The message needs nine rows but the last one is not completely filled. Any two letter are written into the vacant spaces to complete the rectangle.

Here we add 'ab'. It is probably a good idea to avoid adding 'x' or 'z' because they would obviouly be space fillers. The completed rectangle is:

```
m  e  e
t  a  t
t  h  e
c  l  u
b  h  o
u  s  e
t  o  n
i  g  h
t  a  b
```

The final step is to copy the letters from the rectangle, running down the columns:

m t t c b u t i t e a h l h s o g a e t e u o e n h b

This is the transposition. To decipher it, a person has to know that it is a simple transposition with three columns.

The program has a display very similar to that of cipher1 (see Fig. 15), except that there is no box for entering offset. The message is typed into the upper text area. The encipher key is then pressed and the ciphered text appears in the lower text area.

Here is the listing, which shares so many features (such as the thread, the two text areas and the button) with cipher1 that it does not take long to edit that program to produce this one:

```
import java.awt.*;
import javax.swing.*;
import java.awt.event.*;


public class cipher2 extends JApplet implements
ActionListener, Runnable {
```

```
Thread cipherit = null;
String word;
int wordLength;
int gridHeight;
int unfilled;
JTextArea plainText;
JButton encipher;
JTextArea cipherText;
String cipher = "";
boolean enFlag;
String letter;

public void init() {
    Container base = getContentPane();
    FlowLayout arrange = new FlowLayout();
    base.setLayout(arrange);
    plainText = new JTextArea(4, 25);
    plainText.setLineWrap(true);
    base.add(plainText);
    encipher = new JButton("Encipher") ;
    encipher.addActionListener(this);
    base.add(encipher);
    cipherText = new JTextArea(4, 25);
    cipherText.setEditable(false);
    cipherText.setLineWrap(true);
    base.add(cipherText);
    setContentPane(base);
    setBackground(Color.cyan);
}

public void actionPerformed(ActionEvent e) {
    enFlag = false;
    if (e.getActionCommand() == "Encipher") enFlag
= true;
    repaint();
}

public void start() {
    if (cipherit == null) {
    cipherit = new Thread(this);
    cipherit.start();
    }
}

public void stop() {
    if (cipherit != null) cipherit = null;
}

public void run() {
    while (cipherit == Thread.currentThread() ) {
```

```
        if (enFlag == true) {
                String word = plainText.getText();
                word = word.toLowerCase();
                int wordLength = word.length();
                gridHeight = (wordLength / 3) + 1;
                unfilled = 3 - wordLength % 3;
                wordLength = wordLength + unfilled;

                switch(unfilled) {
                case 1 : word = word + "a"; break;
                case 2 : word = word + "ab"; break;
                case 3 : gridHeight = gridHeight - 1;
break;
                }
                for (int j = 0; j < 3; j = j + 1) {
                        for (int k = 0; k < (3 *
gridHeight) ; k = k + 3) {
                                letter = word.substring(j
+ k, j + k + 1);
                                cipher = cipher + letter;
                        }
                }
                cipherText.setText(cipher);
                enFlag = false;
        }
        repaint();
        }
}

public void paint(Graphics g) {
        Graphics2D g2D = (Graphics2D)g;
        plainText.setBackground(Color.lightGray);
        plainText.setForeground(Color.blue);
        encipher.setBackground(Color.red);
        cipherText.setBackground(Color.lightGray);
        cipherText.setForeground(Color.blue);
}}
```

The width is 300 and the height is 250. As usual, we look at the more interesting features of the listing. The first of these is the method for making the text wrap round at the end of a line. In the init() method we apply the setLineWrap() method to the two text areas. The method takes a boolean parameter and we set it to true, to enable line wrapping.

We should have done this for the text areas in *cipher1*, but we left it out to keep the program as short as possible. You may have discovered that the text areas get wider to accommodate a long message. You can see the extension by dragging the right-hand margin of the applet.

As before, the run () method is within a while... loop and the ciphering routine is run subject to the condition that enFlag is true. This ensures that the program waits for us to finish typing in the text and click on the button.

In this program, unlike *cipher1*, it is essential to type the text with no spaces between the words. It is possible to add a routine to ignore spaces as they are typed, but this makes the program longer. However, we do include a line to convert all upper-case letters to lower-case.

The next step is to find out how many rows of three letters the message needs. The number of rows is gridHeight. Having found the length of the text (wordLength), gridHeight is calculated by dividing wordLength by 3. This is integer division which ignores any remainder, so this tells us how many *complete* rows are needed, but does not provide for an unfilled row. So we add one more row to the result of the division.

To find out how many, if any, letters are in the unfilled row, we use modulo division (symbol %). This assigns the value 1, 2 or 3 to the variable unfilled. What we do next depends on the value of unfilled. We could do this by a sequence of conditional statements such as:

```
if (unfilled == 1) { ...
if (unfilled == 2) { ...
if (unfilled == 3) { ...
```

However, there is another way of doing this which makes it easier to see what is happening. We use the switch () method, which takes an integer parameter. In this program we want to switch the action of the program according to the value of the integer variable unfilled. The body of the switch () method comprises three cases, 1, 2, and 3. One of these is selected and acted on, depending on the value of unfilled.

In cases 1 and 2 we fill the unfilled places in the bottom row with "a" or "ab" to complete the row. In case 3 the entire bottom row is unfilled, so we simple cut it off by decrementing gridHeight.

At last we get to the actual transposition. This involves two nested `for...` loops:

Outer loop in which loop variable `j` is incremented from 0 to 3 in steps of 1.

Inner loop in which loop variable `k` is incremented from 0 in steps of 3, stopping after it reaches the bottom line.

Within the inner loop the two loop variables are added together to give the index used with `substring()`. It picks out the corresponding single character from the plain text string. Looking at this operation with our previous example, we can see that, with `j = 0`, the values produced by the addition of `k` are 0, 3, 6, 9, 12, and so on. This picks out the letters of the first column: m, t, t, c, and so on.

When we get to the bottom row, `j` is incremented and now we run down the second column, with the index set to 1, 4, 7, 10, 13 and so on. This picks out e, a, h, l, and the rest of column 2. Finally, with `j` = 2, the program selects the letters from the third column.

As each letter is selected it is added to the `cipher` string. When complete, the cipher is displayed in the `cipherText` text area.

Things to do

1) Write a program, *decipher2*, which accepts the enciphered text and turns it back into plain text.

2) The width of the rectangle is set to three in *cipher2*, when it calculates the value of `gridHeight`. By changing the divisor and changing '3' in the loop conditions, we can alter the width and so produce a different cipher. Modify the listing to work on a width of four or five. Better still, write a routine to allow the required width to be typed in and then used in the enciphering routine.

3) Write a routine to accept plain text with spaces between the words and to delete them before enciphering.

100

Codes for applets

Applets lend themselves to ciphering and deciphering but are less suited to dealing with codes. The main problem is that the codes usually require a code book, in other words an extensive data base. However, there is one example of a code that has its data base built into your computer. This is *Unicode* which in its latest version represents printable characters and a number of printer instructions as code numbers in the range 0 to 131071 (0000 to 1FFFF).

Only the codes with the lower numbers are likely to be in your computer's data base. These always include the codes for printer instructions, alphabetic and numeric characters, and punctuation. They have the same numbers as the earlier and still widely used 7-bit code, the ASCII code. The codes range from 0 to 127 (00 to FF in hexadecimal). Accented characters and characters other than the Roman alphabet (such as ¥ the yen symbol ,which has the code E2D in hexadecimal, (0165 in decimal) follow on from the ASCII characters). They include all sorts of symbols, as you will be able to see when you use the code program, *decode1* (p. 105-6).

Before adventuring further into *Unicode*, here is a programmed routine that has applications in many programs. It validates data entered from the keyboard. In this case the program asks the operator to key in a number between 0 and 9. It accepts input from the keys '0' to '9' but, if the operator keys in an alphabetic character such as 'e', it is rejected.

Here is the listing of *validate*:

```
import java.awt.*;
import javax.swing.*;
import java.awt.event.*;

public class validate extends JApplet implements
KeyListener {

    JTextField input = new JTextField(10);
    int value;
    int unic;
    String message = "Key in a number (0 - 9)";
    String lastMessage = " ";
```

```
public void init() {
    Container base = getContentPane();
    FlowLayout arrange = new FlowLayout();
    base.setLayout(arrange);
    input.addKeyListener(this);
    base.add(input);
    setContentPane(base);
    setBackground(Color.cyan);
}

public void keyPressed(KeyEvent kp) {
    input.setText(" ");
    char num = kp.getKeyChar();
    unic = (int)num;

    if (unic > 41 & unic <58){
            value = unic - 48;
            message = "Key pressed is " + value;
    }
    else message = "Numeric keys only";
    repaint();
}

public void keyReleased(KeyEvent kr) {}
public void keyTyped(KeyEvent kt) {}


public void paint(Graphics g) {
    Graphics2D g2D = (Graphics2D)g;
    input.setBackground(Color.yellow);
    g2D.setColor(Color.cyan);
    g2D.drawString(lastMessage, 5, 50);
    g2D.setColor(Color.black);
    g2D.drawString(message, 5, 50);
    lastMessage = message;
}
}
```

The width of this applet is 250 and its height is 150. The essential
work of this program is done in the keyPressed() method. The
first action on detecting a key press is to clear the text field of any text
that may be there left over from a previous action. Only a single
character can be typed there, so setting the text to a single space clears
the display.

The getKeyChar() method returns a char value, which is assigned
to the char variable, num. The next line casts this into an integer
variable, unic. Now we are ready for the logic.

The numeric characters 0 to 9, have the *Unicodes* 48 to 57. We therefore use an `if...` conditional routine to find out if `unic` is within this range. If so, the number of the key pressed is found by subtracting 48 from the *Unicode* value. This is assigned to the integer, `value`. Following this, we define a message to state that the key pressed is as defined by `value`.

If the key is outside the range 0 to 9, the message is a warning that it is out of range. The graphics display is then repainted to show the message.

The `if...` routine is the point at which other actions can be programmed. It might be that a maths routine uses the value in a calculation. Or we might have two or more `if...` routines to take different actions according to which key is pressed. This could be the basis of selecting between different optional actions.

Here we simply display the outcome, `message`, as shown in the listing of the `paint()` method.

The `paint()` method illustates a useful technique for displaying messages on the same part of the screen without overprinting them. In some other programs we use a rectangle of the same colour as the backgound to blank out the existing message. Here we clear it by overprinting it with itself but in the background colour. Then we display the new message on the cleared space.

The routine uses two strings, `message` (the current message) and `lastMessage` (the message before the current one). Before printing the new message, the last message is printed in background colour. Having done this, the value of `lastMessage` is updated to the value of `message`, ready to clear the display when the next message is to be displayed.

This routine can, of course be set with a smaller single-digit range, such as 1-3. It can also be used to verify an alphabetic range such as A-D. To extend it to double-digits requires a little extra programming, as is seen in the next example.

103

Exploring Unicode

This program, *decode1* lets you look through the Unicode codebook that is already stored in your computer — even if you are not sure whereabouts and how extensive it is. It is mainly an adaptation of the listing of *validate*, so the easiest way to obtain it is to begin by loading that program and extend it.

The program is also of interest as an illustration of how to validate numeric input that has two or more digits. In Fig. 16 it is verifying that the entry consists only of numerals and that their value is within the range 0 to 65535. This covers the whole of the *Unicode* range except for the more recent additions of *Unicode 4*, which are not likely to be on your computer unless you have specialist software.

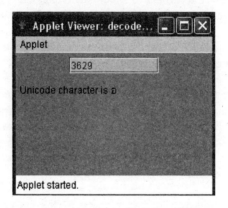

Fig. 16. The decode1 *program has validated an entry of 3629 and displays the decoded character from the Thai alphabet.*

When you have tried out this program, you could go back to the *cipher1* and other enciphering and deciphering programs and add a method to validate the entry procedure so that it accepts only alphabetic characters and spaces. In the case of *cipher2*, it should reject spaces.

Here is the listing of *decode1*:

```
import java.awt.*;
import javax.swing.*;
import java.awt.event.*;

public class decode1 extends JApplet implements
KeyListener {

    JTextField input = new JTextField(10);
    int value;
    int unic;
    int codeNum;
    char code;
    String message = "Key in a number (0 - 65535)";
    String lastMessage = " ";
    String codeText;


public void init() {
    Container base = getContentPane();
    FlowLayout arrange = new FlowLayout();
    base.setLayout(arrange);
    input.addKeyListener(this);
    base.add(input);
    setContentPane(base);
    setBackground(Color.cyan);
}

public void keyPressed(KeyEvent kp) {

    char num = kp.getKeyChar();
    unic = (int)num;

    if (unic > 41 & unic <58){
            value = unic - 48;
            message = "Key pressed is " + value;
            }
    else if (unic == 10){
            String codeText = input.getText();
            codeNum = Integer.parseInt(codeText);
            if (codeNum > 65535) message = "Code out
of range";
                    else {code = (char)codeNum;
                    message = "Unicode character is
" + code;
                    }
            }
    else message = "Numeric keys only";
    repaint();
}
```

```
public void keyReleased(KeyEvent kr) {}
public void keyTyped(KeyEvent kt) {}

public void paint(Graphics g) {
    Graphics2D g2D = (Graphics2D)g;
    input.setBackground(Color.yellow);
    g2D.setColor(Color.cyan);
    g2D.drawString(lastMessage, 5, 50);
    g2D.setColor(Color.black);
    g2D.drawString(message, 5, 50);
    lastMessage = message;
}
}
```

The width is 250 and the height is 150. Validation of a multi-digit entry is tackled by first verifying the individual digits as they are typed in, then checking that the whole number is within the range. The 'Enter' key is to be pressed to indicate when the entry is complete.

The whole routine is contained in the keyPressed() method. The first statement there obtains the char value of the key pressed, calling it num. This is cast as an integer called unic. We then work with unic, folowing the same technique as in *validate*, to check that the key has a value from 0 to 9. If it has, the value is displayed, but when using this routine in your own programs you could make something else happen instead.

As mentioned above, pressing the 'Enter' key indicates that all digits have been keyed in. Pressing the 'Enter' key generates *Unicode* that causes a line feed (a printer jumps to the beginning of the next line). This entry is processed by the else if... statement. We first use getText() to read the text that has been entered in the text field, and call this codeText. This is a string, but is converted into its numeric equivalent by Integer.parseInt(), and called codeNum.

We now examine codeNum to confirm that it is not greater than 65535. It can not be less than 0 since keying in a minus symbol is rejected. If it is greater than 65535, the 'Out of range' message is displayed.

If it is within range, `code`, the *Unicode* character corresponding to `codeNum`, is found by casting `code` into its char equivalent and is displayed in a message.

Finally, if the keyed entry is neither a numeral nor the 'Enter' key, the "Numeric keys only" is displayed.

When you have compiled the listing, run it and try entering different values. Some may give a small square symbol because there is no *Unicode* character of that value or your computer does not have it in its 'code book'.

Try low values to obtain alphanumeric characters and punctuation. Slightly higher values give an assortment of accented letters of various European languages, and various other symbols, such as the backslash (\ ) for 92. Higher again, we find characters such as the Thai one obtained in Fig. 16 by entering unicode 3629. Try some even larger values. For example, 10145 gives a right-pointing arrow.

To enter another number use the backspace key to clear the existing entry. You will be advised to enter numeric keys only, but ignore this.

10 Logical lamps

The programs and routines in this chapter are not intended to be run on their own. They are to be incorporated into applets that you design yourself. Their purpose is to make your applets more attractive to the eye.

Because you will probably want to put them in *Java 2* applets, these routines have all been written for *Java 2*. However, all but the last one can be easily converted to *Java 1*, as explained on pp. 187-193.

The word 'lamps' in the title of this chapter is not to be taken literally. Instead of switching on physical lamps, electronic or otherwise, we display patches of bright colours on the computer screen. Usually the patches are circular discs, but there is no reason why they can not be of any other shape. If you have been studying the *Java Digest* and the end of the book, you may have seen *digest 11*, which simulates the action of a traffic signal. It lights red, amber and green 'lamps' according to the conventional sequence. This action is controlled by the logical statements in the program, so we have 'logical lamps'.

Flashing lamps

A lamp that is flashing on and off at a fairly rapid rate catches the eye much more readily than a lamp that is continuously switched on. The *colourflash* program below does just this.

Here is the listing:

```java
import java.awt.*;
import java.awt.geom.*;
import javax.swing.*;

public class colourflash extends JApplet implements
Runnable {

Thread flashit = null;
boolean flash = false;

public void init() {

    Container base = getContentPane();
    setContentPane(base);
    setBackground(Color.gray);
}

public void start() {
    if (flashit == null) flashit = new Thread(this);
    flashit.start();
    }

public void stop() {
    if (flashit == null) flashit = null;
    }

public void run() {
    while (flashit == Thread.currentThread() ) {
            flash = true;
            repaint();
            try {Thread.sleep(1000); }
            catch(InterruptedException e) {}
            flash = false;
            repaint();
            try {Thread.sleep(1000); }
            catch(InterruptedException e) {}
}}

public void paint(Graphics g) {
    Graphics2D g2D = (Graphics2D)g;
    Ellipse2D.Float lamp = new Ellipse2D.Float(100F,
100F, 40F, 40F);

    if (flash == true) g2D.setColor(Color.red);
    else g2D.setColor(Color.blue);
    g2D.fill(lamp);
}}
```

The width is 240 and the height is 250. As listed on p. 109, a circular disc is displayed in the centre of the screen. It changes colour from red to blue and back to red again, repeating every 2 seconds.

Timing is controlled by a thread, flashit. In the run() method we can see that the boolean variable flash is made true for 1 second, then made false for 1 second. When flash is true, the drawing colour in paint() is set to red. Otherwise, the colour is set to blue. Note that in run() the repaint() method is called each time the value of flash is changed.

This routine is easily adaptable to whatever flashing action you prefer. As listed, the colour alternates between red and blue. But you can use any other pair of colours instead. Or one of the colours can be the same as the background colour. In this case the lamp appears simply to flash on and off.

The rate of flashing can be made faster or slower by changing the parameter of the sleep() method. You can also alter the duty cycle, the ratio between the time spent showing red and the time spent in blue. So, for example, if the first sleep() is for 100 ms and the second for 1900 ms, it still flashes at the same rate as before but would show blue most of the time with a brief flash of red every 2 seconds.

Finally, the lamp can be any shape such as an ellipse, a rectangle, a line, or a complex shape drawn with GeneralPath(). And, of course, it could also be a text string. Since it can be adapted in so many ways, *colourflash* is a useful applet to apply to your own designs.

Fading the colours

Instead of switching instantly from one colour to another, we can make the change a slow one. This subtle change or *fade*, as it would be called by cinema buffs, is another way of attracting attention.

The *colourfade* program fades the colour of a disc from red, through shades of purple to blue, and then back through purples to red.

The main difference from *colour flash* is in the run() method. Because we need to mix the colours gradually, predefined colours are no use. Instead we mix the colour from the three primary colours, using the Color (*int, int, int*) method. In this, the three arguments specify the levels of red, green and blue in the mixture. Levels can range from 0 (no colour) to 255 (saturation).

In this program the colours fade from saturated red to saturated blue and the run() method achieves this by two for... loops.

The first loop produces the fade from blue to red. At the start of the loop, when j = 0, redval has the value 0 and blueval is 255. The colour mix is pure blue. As the loop repeats, redval increases by 1 and blueval decreases by 1 every 5 ms. The colour varies through shades of purple. At the end, redval is 255 and blueval is 0. The colour is pure red. The second loop produces the opposite effect. Blue increases to saturation while red fades to zero.

The listing of *colourfade* is a reasonably short one:

```
import java.awt.*;
import java.awt.geom.*;
import javax.swing.*;

public class colourfade extends JApplet implements
Runnable {

Thread fadeit = null;
int redval;
int blueval;;

public void init() {
     Container base = getContentPane();
     setContentPane(base);
     setBackground(Color.gray);
}

public void start() {
     if (fadeit == null) fadeit = new Thread(this);
     fadeit.start();
     }

public void stop() {
     if (fadeit != null) fadeit = null;
     }
```

```
public void run() {
    while (fadeit == Thread.currentThread() ) {
            for (int j = 0; j < 255; j = j + 1) {
            redval = j; blueval = 255 - j;
            repaint();

            try {Thread.sleep(5); }
            catch(InterruptedException e) {}
            }
            for (int j = 0; j < 255; j = j + 1) {
            redval = 255 - j; blueval = j;
            repaint();

            try {Thread.sleep(5); }
            catch(InterruptedException e) {}
            }
}}

public void paint(Graphics g) {
    Graphics2D g2D = (Graphics2D)g;
    Ellipse2D.Float lamp = new
  Ellipse2D.Float(100F, 100F, 40F, 40F);
    Color faded = new Color(redval, 0, blueval);
    g2D.setColor(faded);
    g2D.fill(lamp);
}}
```

The width is 240 and the height is 250. The graphics() method is
straightforward. A circular ellipse, lamp, is defined. Then a new
colour, faded, is created using the two parameters, redval and
blueval that were assigned values in run(). Finally, lamp is
drawn on the screen, in its new colour, replacing the previous version.

Like *colourflash*, this routine can also be used with other shapes and
when drawing lines of text. To illustrate this point, the program in the
next section is a version that upgrades *colourflash* with full *Swing*
graphics.

Filling out the graphics

While admiring the flashing effect of *colourflash* we wondered how it
would look in a real-life application. So we reloaded it, rewrote the
paint() method, and called the new program *colourstar*. Opposite
is the listing of paint().The rest is the same as in *colourflash*. Or it
could be the same as *colourfade*.

```
public void paint(Graphics g) {
    Graphics2D g2D = (Graphics2D)g;

    g2D.setColor(Color.blue);
    BasicStroke wideline = new BasicStroke(10);
    g2D.setStroke(wideline);
    RoundRectangle2D.Float border = new
 RoundRectangle2D.Float(20F,  20F,  420F,  260F,  20F,  20F,
20F);
    g2D.draw(border);

    GeneralPath star;
    BasicStroke starline = new BasicStroke(8,
 BasicStroke.CAP_BUTT, BasicStroke.JOIN_MITER, 10);
    star = new GeneralPath();
    star.moveTo(150F, 60F);
    star.lineTo(160F, 210F);
    star.lineTo(50F, 100F);
    star.lineTo(200F, 80F);
    star.lineTo(100F, 200F);
    star.closePath();
    if (flash == true) g2D.setColor(Color.red);
    else g2D.setColor(Color.blue);
    g2D.draw(star);

    g2D.setColor(Color.yellow);
    Font    starfont    =    new    Font("SansSerif",
Font.ITALIC, 48);
    g2D.setFont(starfont);
    g2D.drawString("Bargains!", 200, 180);
}}
```

The width is 470 and the height is 300. The method defines the features of the star. First the width of a line, `wideline`, is defined by using `BasicStroke()`. Then a rectangle with rounded corners is drawn to make a blue border a little way in from the edges of the screen.

To produce the star we use `GeneralPath`, first defining a new line, `starline`, slighly narrower than wideline and using several more parameters. The line has butt ends and mitre joins, with a limit of 10 on their length. This will give the figure a 'spiky' look because all the angles are sharp ones. This is ideal for drawing a star.

The star shape is defined as a closed path with five segments. The shape is deliberately irregular to give it an informal look.

The drawing colour for the star is set to red or blue according to the state of flash, the boolean flag variable in the run(() method. The star is then drawn in the current colour and flashes from blue to red and back again with a period of 2 s.

To complete the display, a new font, starfont is instantiated. It is one of the standard fonts, a sans serif italic font being suitable for this kind of display. The font size is 48 pixels.

Fig. 17 shows how it looks on the screen (but the bright primary colours and the flashing star give it much more life).

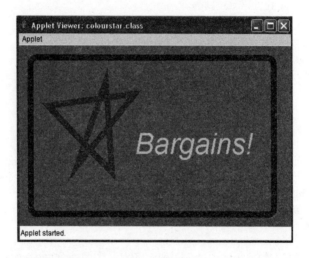

Fig. 17. An eyecatching panel displayed by the colourstar *version of* colourflash.

Planning a display sequence

Although lightning is not a lamp, it is one of the most powerful sources of light operating on Earth. This program simulates a lightning storm. If you can obtain an audio clip, the effect can be enhanced with some bursts of thunder.

For obvious reasons the program is called *umbrella*. When developing it, we built on the programming of *colourflash* — after all, lightning flashes vividly, as we shall see.

The complete listing of *umbrella* is:

```java
import java.awt.*;
import java.awt.geom.*;
import javax.swing.*;
import java.net.*;
import java.applet.*;

public class umbrella extends JApplet implements
Runnable {

Thread flashit = null;
boolean flash = false;
boolean sky = false;
boolean thunder = false;
boolean message = false;
URL thunfile;
AudioClip soundfx;

public void init() {

    Container base = getContentPane();
    setContentPane(base);
    setBackground(Color.black);
    soundfx       =       getAudioClip(getCodeBase(),
"thunderd.wav");
}

public void start() {

    if (flashit == null) flashit = new Thread(this);
    flashit.start();
    }

}
```

```java
public void stop() {

    if (flashit == null) flashit = null;


public void run() {

    while (flashit == Thread.currentThread() ) {
            flash = false; sky = false; thunder =
false; message = false;
            repaint();
            try {Thread.sleep(5000); }
            catch(InterruptedException e) {}

            for (int j = 0; j < 8; j = j + 1) {
            if (j > 3) message = true;
            else message = false;
            flash = true; sky = false;
            repaint();
            try {Thread.sleep(50); }
            catch(InterruptedException e) {}
            flash = false; sky = true;
            repaint();
            try {Thread.sleep(50); }
            catch(InterruptedException e) {}
            }

            flash = false; sky = false;thunder =
true; message = true;
            repaint();
            try {Thread.sleep(5000); }
            catch(InterruptedException e) {}

}}

public void paint(Graphics g) {

    Graphics2D g2D = (Graphics2D)g;

    if (flash == false) setBackground(Color.black);
    else setBackground(Color.white);
    if (sky == false) setBackground(Color.black);
    else setBackground(Color.white);

    if (thunder == true) soundfx.play();
    if (thunder == false) soundfx.stop();
    if (message == true) g2D.setColor(Color.yellow);
    else g2D.setColor(Color.black);
```

116

```
GeneralPath shaft;
    BasicStroke shaftline = new BasicStroke(8, Ba-
sicStroke.CAP_BUTT, BasicStroke.JOIN_MITER, 10);
    g2D.setStroke(shaftline);
    shaft = new GeneralPath();
    shaft.moveTo(100F, 10F);
    shaft.lineTo(150F, 80F);
    shaft.lineTo(180F, 170F);
    shaft.lineTo(50F, 80F);
    shaft.lineTo(140F, 250F);
    shaft.lineTo(110, 290);
    if (flash == true) g2D.setColor(Color.white);
    else g2D.setColor(Color.black);
    g2D.draw(shaft);

    if (message == true) g2D.setColor(Color.yellow);
    else g2D.setColor(Color.black);
    Font    starfont    =    new    Font("SansSerif",
Font.ITALIC, 48);
    g2D.setFont(starfont);
    g2D.drawString("Take your", 200, 180);
    g2D.drawString("umbrella!", 200, 220);
}}
```

The width is 470 and the height is 300.The program consists of four
items: lightning flash, sky (background), sound of thunder and a
message. These are to be displayed (or heard) in a predefined sequence. The sequence is best described by a table:

Phase	Lightning	Sky	Thunder	Message
1 Initial wait of 5 s.	F	F	F	F
2 Lightning flashes	T/F	F/T	F	F, later T
3 Thunder	F	F	T	T
4 Final	F	F	T	T

F = false, T = true

117

This sequence is controlled by the run() method, which assigns the values F or T to the four boolean flag variables (see the global list). The values of the variables are used in the paint() method to determine when and how each item is displayed or heard.

For each item the flag values are:

Lightning: Flash white when true, black when false. A loop alternates the flag between F and T during Phase 2 only. The sleep periods are short to give the effect of flashes of lightning.

Sky: Flash white when true, black when false. The same loop alternates the flag in the same way as the flash flag but in the opposite sense. The effect is a white flash on a black sky, alternating with a kind of after-image of a black flash on a white sky.

Thunder: The flag starts the audio clip in Phase 3, when it becomes true. Because it was called by soundfx.play(), the sound continues until the audio clip has played once. It continues, if necessary, through to Phase 4. However, if it has not already ended, it is stopped at the end of Phase 4 by calling soundfx.stop(). In some audio clips there is a delay after starting before the thunder is heard. This may mean changing the flag to true earlier than in this listing. The aim is for the thunder to begin a fraction of a second after the lightning has ended.

Message: The flag is true for Phases 2 to 4. It begins the third time the loop is run, and is displayed in yellow. It appears during the storm but is not clearly legible until Phase 4, when it is seen against a black sky for 5 s.

The description above explains the intentions of the programmer when writing the run() and paint() methods. You may have different ideas on what a thunderstorm is like. Adapt the sequence of flag-setting to suit your ideas — it's all a matter of logic!

To run this program you will need a short sound clip of thunder, recorded in the .wav format.

The effect is so striking (*sic*) that no illustration on the pages of a book can do it justice. Key it in and run it!

Changing shape

The previous routines have all been concerned with changing colours, but there are other features of an image that can be changed. One of these is its shape. For example, when we create an ellipse, we are able to set its width and height and so set its shape. In the previous routines the width and height were made equal to produce a circular disc. Now we vary them to produce a shape-changing ellipse.

The routine is called *shaper*, and here is its listing:

```
import java.awt.*;
import java.awt.geom.*;
import javax.swing.*;

public class shaper extends JApplet implements
Runnable {

Thread shape = null;
float wval;
float hval;
float lastwval;
float lasthval;

public void init() {

    Container base = getContentPane();
    setContentPane(base);
    setBackground(Color.gray);
}

public void start() {
    if (shape == null) shape = new Thread(this);
    shape.start();
    }

public void stop() {
    if (shape != null) shape = null;
    }
```

```
public void run() {
    while (shape == Thread.currentThread() ) {
        for (int j = 50; j < 101; j = j + 1) {
        wval = j; hval = 150 - j;
        repaint();

        try {Thread.sleep(5); }
        catch(InterruptedException e) {}
        }
        for (int j = 50; j < 101; j = j + 1) {
        hval = j; wval = 150 - j;
        repaint();

        try {Thread.sleep(5); }
        catch(InterruptedException e) {}
        }
}}

public void paint(Graphics g) {
    Graphics2D g2D = (Graphics2D)g;
    Ellipse2D.Float lamp = new Ellipse2D.Float(125 -
wval/2, 125 - hval/2, wval, hval);
    Ellipse2D.Float lastlamp = new
Ellipse2D.Float(125 - lastwval/2, 125 - lasthval/2,
lastwval, lasthval);
    g2D.setColor(Color.gray);
    g2D.fill(lastlamp);
    g2D.setColor(Color.green);
    g2D.fill(lamp);
    lastwval = wval;
    lasthval = hval;
}}
```

The width is 240 and the height is 250. The global variables are all declared as floats because float values are required for defining ellipses. Note that wval and hval are the current width and height of the ellipse; their previous values are defined by lastwval and lasthval. These 'last' values are used when blanking out the previously displayed ellipse before displaying the current one.

The shape is changed in run(). A for... loop increases width from 50 to 100, while decreasing height from 100 to 50. The effect is a broad flat elliipse gradually becoming a tall thin ellipse. Each step takes 5 ms, so the whole process takes 250 ms.

The second for... loop reverses this action.

In `paint()`, the `lamp` and `lastlamp` ellipses are created using the appropriate pair of width and height parameters. Then the image of the previous ellipse is cleared by overprinting it with `lastlamp` in the background colour. The current `lamp` is printed in green.

The 'last' values are updated to the current values and the cycle repeats in `run()`, which sets the new values for the ellipse.

Travelling lights

One of the attractive features of fairground stalls is the array of lights that appear to run all round the edges of the booths. More recently we have seen strings of travelling lights decorating houses at Christmas.

This *traveller* routine shows how to simulate travelling lights by displaying a row of small yellow (when 'on') squares that appears to move across the screen. In this version, the lamps are 'on' in pairs, separated by a pair of 'off' lamps. The 'off' lamps are the same colour as the background. Other sequences are programmed simply by altering the values in the template array.

The listing shows the array to contain {0, 0, 1, 1}. Value '0' means 'lamp off', and '1' means 'lamp on'.

This sequence of four values is displayed as a horizontal row of four squares on the left of the screen. The same four squares are repeated four places to the right and so on across the screen. The display then is equivalent to:

$$0\ 0\ 1\ 1\ 0\ 0\ 1\ 1\ 0\ 0\ 1\ 1\ 0\ 0\ 1\ 1\ ...$$

To obtain the illusion of motion this display is replaced by:

$$1\ 0\ 0\ 1\ 1\ 0\ 0\ 1\ 1\ 0\ 0\ 1\ 1\ 0\ 0\ 1\ ...$$

And then by:

$$1\ 1\ 0\ 0\ 1\ 1\ 0\ 0\ 1\ 1\ 0\ 0\ 1\ 1\ 0\ 0\ ...$$

And finally by:

$$0\ 1\ 1\ 0\ 0\ 1\ 1\ 0\ 0\ 1\ 1\ 0\ 0\ 1\ 1\ 0\ ...$$

The next move takes the display back to its original state.

The pattern of lights on and off is stored in an array called template. This has four index positions, 0 to 3. This is defined as a global variable. In the listing the pattern is 0011, but it could be 0001 for example or any other combination of 0's and 1's.

The method prints this pattern, in the form of rectangles that are either grey (=0, off) or yellow (=1, off). This is done in the inner loop, loop variable k. The outer loop repeats this action 20 times, printing each succesive pattern four 'lamps' to the right.

To animate the display we replace the pattern in template with a shifted pattern, 1001. This is done in the run() method. The action is similar to the assembler instruction for a shift register in a microprocessor, 'rotate right with carry'. Fig 18 shows what happens.

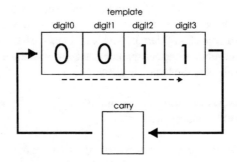

Fig. 18. The pattern of digits in template *is*
rotated to the right, through the carry *variable.*

The order of moving the digits is important. The content of digit3 is first moved to the carry. Then starting with digit2, the content of digit2 is moved to digit3, then digit1 to digit2, and digit0 to digit1. Finally, the content of carry is moved to digit0. The pattern is now '1001'.

This pattern is displayed 20 times across the screen and the whole string of lamps appears to have shifted one step to the right. Every 0.1 s, run() shifts the pattern and the apparent motion continues.

The listing is:

```
import java.awt.*;
import java.awt.geom.*;
import javax.swing.*;


public class traveller extends JApplet implements
Runnable {

Thread travel = null;

float xDist;
int template[] = {0, 0, 1, 1};
int carry = 1;
int origin;

public void init() {

    Container base = getContentPane();
    setContentPane(base);
    setBackground(Color.gray);
}

public void start() {
    if (travel == null) travel = new Thread(this);
    travel.start();
    }

public void stop() {
    if (travel != null) travel = null;
    }

public void run() {
    while (travel == Thread.currentThread() ) {
            carry = template[3];
            for (int j = 3;j > 0; j = j - 1) {
            template[j] = template[j - 1]; }
            template[0] = carry;
            repaint();

            try {Thread.sleep(100); }
            catch(InterruptedException e) {}
            }
}

public void paint(Graphics g) {
    Graphics2D g2D = (Graphics2D)g;

    for (int j = 10; j < 250; j = j + 40) {
            origin = j;
}
```

```
            for (int k = 0; k < 4; k = k + 1) {
            if (template[k] == 0)
g2D.setColor(Color.gray);
            else g2D.setColor(Color.yellow);
            xDist = origin + (10 * k);
            Rectangle2D.Float lamp = new
  Rectangle2D.Float(xDist, 50, 8, 8);
            g2D.fill(lamp);
            }
}}
```

The width is 260 and the height is 150.

This routine can be used to produce a decorative border or underlining in an advertising applet. The routine can be adapted to a vertical row of light by operating on yDist instead of on xDist. By operating on both at the same time you can make the lamps travel on a diagonal.

Further programming can produce lamps that change colour periodically. You could adapt run() to reverse the direction of travel every so often. One useful extension is to make the lamps travel in a circle. As we see in the next section, this is only a matter of adapting the paint() method.

A ring of lamps

Java has a large number of maths functions, most of which we have never used in this book. Here is the chance to put two of these to work. Given the size of an angle, the function Math.sin(float) produces the sine of the angle. The float is the size of the angle, in radians. Similarly, Math.cos(float) produces the cosine. Fig,. 19 shows how we use these two functions to make our lamps spin in a circle.

The program repeats the pattern of lamps 20 times in the complete circle. As there are 6.28 rad in a circle, the angle for each pattern of four lamps is 6.28/20 = 0.314 rad. Within the pattern, the angle between one lamp and its neighbour is 0.314/4 = 0.0785 rad.

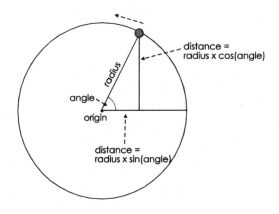

distance =
radius x cos(angle)

radius

angle

origin

distance =
radius x sin(angle)

*Fig. 19. As the object circles around the origin, its
horizontal and vertical distances from the origin (centre of
circle) vary as the sine and cosine of the angle.*

The position of each lamp is given by the coordinates its top left
corner, in the case of a rectangle. For ellipses it is the corner of the
imaginary rectangle that just encloses the ellipse. The x coordinate is
calculated from:

   x coordinate of the origin + x-distance of lamp from the origin
 = x coordinate of the origin + (radius × sin(angle))

This translates into the expression in the listing:

```
xDist = originx + (radius *
(float)(Math.sin(angle)));
```

Similarly for the y coordinate. As the angle increases from 0 to 6.28
the sines and cosines in certain quadrants are negative, so the lamps
are positioned to the left and/or above the origin. Fig 20   overleaf
shows the resulting circle of lamps.

All that remains is to draw some bold text or display an image inside
the circle. Try a short phrase such as "Sale Price", or "Happy
Birthday" in a bold, informal font, size 48.

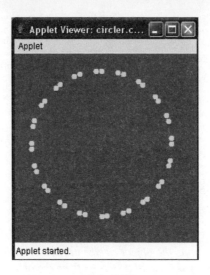

*Fig. 20. A whirling circle of lamps
produced by* circler.

The listing of *circler* is much the same as that of *traveller*. It is just the geometry that differs. You can easily produce the listing by editing the traveller file:

1) Change the class name from traveller to circler.

2) To the global variables, add:

```
float yDist;
float originx;   (replacing int origin;)
float originy;
double radius = 100;
```

3 Replace the existing paint () method with the following:

```
    public void paint(Graphics g) {
        Graphics2D g2D = (Graphics2D)g;

        originx = 120F;
        originy = 120F;
```

126

```
for (int j = 0; j < 20; j = j + 1) {
            for (int k = 0; k < 4; k = k + 1) {
            if (template[k] == 0)
g2D.setColor(Color.gray);
            else g2D.setColor(Color.yellow);
            angle = (0.314 * j) + (0.0785 * k);
            xDist = originx + (radius *
(float)(Math.sin(angle)));
            yDist = originy + (radius *
(float)(Math.cos(angle)));
            Ellipse2D.Float lamp = new
 Ellipse2D.Float(xDist, yDist, 8, 8);
            g2D.fill(lamp);
            }
}}}
```

The width and height of this applet are 260.

A handy utility program

This program is called *eggtimer* because it can be set to time the period for boiling an egg. But it can be set to flash its lamp and sound the alert after any reaonable period. It can time moves in games such as Chess, or time the steak cooking on the barbecue.

The applet has a display consisting of two buttons and a 'lamp'. The lamp is a circular patch, which is grey when off and red when on.. Fig. 21, overleaf, shows how it looks.

The operation of a timer has four phases, so the best way to tackle the sequencing of the run() method is to draw out the table shown overleaf.

There are two threads in this program. The "cook" thread times the cooking period. The "flash" thread alternately makes the flashFlag true and false. We run this thread all the time though it has an effect only when the lamp is on.

127

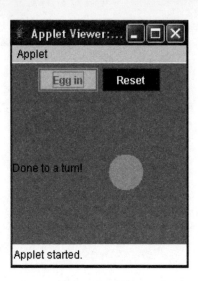

Fig. 21. The egg timer displays its flashing lamp (disc on right) and a message when the time is up.

The "cook" thread is instantiated in start() as usual but it is not started there, unlike most other programs. The result is that in Phase 1 (see table, opposite) the program waits for the "Egg in" button to be pressed. At first, when the first while... loop is run, cook is not a current thread, so the content of the loop is by-passed. At this stage, the same applies to the second while... loop.

Nothing happens until the actionPerformed() method detects an event in the form of one of the buttons being pressed. If it identifies the source as the "Egg in" button, it starts the cook thread. Now the first loop in run() comes into effect. The cooking flag is made true and there is a sleep delay while the egg is cooked.

In the listing (opposite), the delay period is set to 10 s for the purposes of a demonstration. For cooking eggs, the period should be 60000 for every minute, making 300000 for a 5-minute egg.

Phase	Cooking flag	Done flag	Lamp	Message
1 Waiting	F	F	Off	No message
2 Egg in pan	T	F	On	Cooking now
3 Time up	F	T	Flashing	Done to a turn!
4 Reset	F	F	Off	No message

The table summarises the phases of the timing loop, showing the state of the flags at each phase.

At the end of the first while... loop the cooking flag is made false and the done flag made true. This puts the program into Phase 3. In paint() the if (done == true) conditional turns the lamp on (red) if flashFlag is true and off (light grey). In fact, flashFlag is alternating all the time and it only requires done to be true to start the flashing.

The last phase is entered when a keypress of "Reset" is detected. The cooking and done flags become false and a new cook thread is instantiated. The time is back to Phase 1, ready to time the next egg.

The listing is:

```
import java.awt.*;
import java.awt.geom.*;
import java.awt.event.*;
import javax.swing.*;
```

```java
public class eggtimer extends JApplet implements
ActionListener, Runnable {

    JButton eggin = new JButton("Egg in");
    JButton reset = new JButton("Reset");
    Thread cook = null;
    Thread flash = null;
    boolean cooking = false;
    boolean done = false;
    boolean flashFlag = false;

public void init() {

    Container timer = getContentPane();
    FlowLayout dial = new FlowLayout();
    timer.setLayout(dial);
    timer.add(eggin);
    eggin.addActionListener(this);
    timer.add(reset);
    reset.addActionListener(this);
    setContentPane(timer);
    setBackground(Color.green);
    }

public void start() {
    if (cook == null) cook = new Thread(this);
    if (flash == null) flash = new Thread(this);
    flash.start();
    }

public void stop() {
    if (cook != null) cook = null;
    if (flash != null) flash = null;
    }

public void run() {
    while ( cook == Thread.currentThread() )
    {
            cooking = true;
            done = false;
            repaint();
            try {Thread.sleep(10000); }
            catch(InterruptedException e) {}
            cooking = false;
            done = true;
            cook.stop();
            repaint();
            }
```

```
      while (flash == Thread.currentThread() )
      {       flashFlag = true;
              repaint();
              try {Thread.sleep(500); }
              catch(InterruptedException e) {}
              flashFlag = false;
              repaint();
              try {Thread.sleep(500); }
              catch(InterruptedException e) {}
      }
}
public void actionPerformed(ActionEvent e) {

      if (e.getActionCommand() == "Egg in") {
              cook.start();
              }
      if (e.getActionCommand() == "Reset") {
              cooking = false;
              done = false;
              cook = new Thread(this);
              }
      repaint();
}

public void paint (Graphics g) {
      Graphics2D g2D = (Graphics2D)g;

      eggin.setForeground(Color.green);
      eggin.setBackground(Color.yellow);
      reset.setForeground(Color.white);
      reset.setBackground(Color.blue);

      g2D.setColor(Color.green);
      Rectangle2D.Float blankit = new
 Rectangle2D.Float(0F, 110F, 100F, 20F);
      g2D.fill(blankit);
      Ellipse2D.Float lamp = new Ellipse2D.Float(110F,
100F, 40F, 40F);
      if (cooking == true) {
      g2D.setColor(Color.blue);
      g2D.drawString("Cooking now", 0, 120);
      g2D.setColor(Color.red);
      g2D.fill(lamp);
      }
      g2D.setColor(Color.lightGray);
      if (done == true & flashFlag == true)
      g2D.setColor(Color.red);
      g2D.fill(lamp);
      if (done == true) {
              g2D.setColor(Color.blue);
              g2D.drawString("Done to a turn!", 0,
120);
                                     }
} }
```

The width and height of the applet are both 200. This program provides several opportunities for enhancements. One obvious addition is an audible alert to sound when cooking is finished. To provide this you need an audio clip saved in the same folder as the program. The clip could be a siren or other alert tone. Or it could be a snatch of music — or even a voice recording saying "Your egg is cooked."

The listing needs only a few additions:

1) To the list of imports, add:
```
import java.net.*;
import java,applet.*;
```

2) To the list of global variables, add:
```
AudioClip soundfx;
```

3) in `actionPerformed()` after `cook = new...` add:
```
soundfx.stop();
```

4) In `paint()`, after the line `g2D,drawString ("Done ...,` add:
```
soundfx = getAudioClip(getCodeBase(),
"file:ALERT.wav");
soundfx.loop();
```

The use of the `loop();` method means that the clip is played repeatedly instead of only once (see p. 170). The alert continues until the reset button is pressed.

Another useful enhancement is to accept a number within a given range to allow the length of the sleep period to be set. Try programming this and use *validate* (p. 101) to check the input.

Further suggestions that you might program are to display either the time elapsed, or the time remaining, every minute.

11 Applet games

To complete the book, we present a selection of short but challenging computer games. They are not as elaborate as the games purchased as a CD but, because you type them in yourself, you have the chance to customise them in ways that are not available with the typical commercial game. So you get you own personalised and unique game (more about that later!) and at the same time learn a little more and understand a little more about *Java* applets.

Cat 'n' Mouse

This is a chase-and-capture game, as might be expected from its title.

The screen is filled with a large blue square which represents a room. In the bottom right corner is a black disc, which is the mouse's hole. At the bottom left of the screen is an orange disc. This is the ginger cat, which is hunting the mouse. To avoid confusion in the description we refer to the mouse as Mickey, and to the computer's mouse simply as the mouse.

The game begins with the appearance of Mickey (grey disc) at the top of the screen. When running the program in some browsers you may need to click the mouse to start the game.

Your task as cat is to catch Mickey before he can reach his hole and disappear into it. This is not as easy as it might sound for Mickey pursues a very erratic route, homing on his hole only gradually.

You steer the cat by using the mouse to position the cursor and then clicking the button. This is not the same as dragging with the button held down. For instance, if you position the cursor above and to the right of the cat, then click, the cat runs toward the upper and right-hand walls.

After the click the cat continues to run in the same direction. Click again to change its direction. If it hits a wall it 'bounces' off. If it manages to get very close to Mickey, the message "Mouse caught!" is displayed and the game ends in victory for the cat.

If Mickey manages to avoid capture and reaches his hole, he has won the game and a message appears, saying "Mouse escapes".

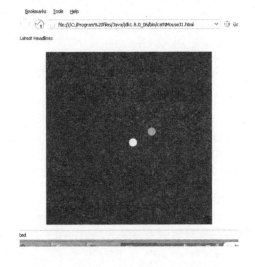

Fig. 22. The Cat 'n' Mouse *game running in* Firefox. *The mousehole is at the bottom right corner. The cat (centre) is almost in striking range of Mickey.*

Because the graphics are very simple the listing (below) is based on *Java 1*. This helps to reduce the length of the listing and also makes the program easier to follow.

```java
import java.awt.*;
import java.applet.*;

public class catNMouseJ1 extends Applet implements
Runnable {

int xDist = 30;
int yDist = 370;
int mxDist = 30;
int myDist = 30;
int cxDist = 0;
int cyDist = 0;
int xinc = 0;
int yinc = 0;
int mDir = 0;
Thread frenzy = null;
boolean holeFlag = false;
boolean caughtFlag = false;

public void init() {
    setBackground(Color.blue);
}

public boolean mouseDown(Event e, int cxDist, int
cyDist ) {
    if (cxDist > xDist) xinc = 5;
    if (cxDist < xDist) xinc =  -5;
    if (cyDist < yDist) yinc = -5;
    if (cyDist > yDist) yinc = 5;
    repaint();
    return true;
}

public void start() {
    if (frenzy == null & holeFlag == false) {
            frenzy = new Thread(this);
            frenzy.start();
}}

public void stop() {
    if (frenzy != null) frenzy = null;
}
```

```java
public void run() {
    while (frenzy == Thread.currentThread() ) {
    if (caughtFlag == false) {
            mDir = (int)(Math.random() * 4);
            if (mxDist > 15 & mxDist < 385 & myDist
>15 & myDist < 385) {
                    if (mDir == 0 & mxDist < 370)
mxDist = mxDist + 15;
                    else if (mDir == 1 & myDist <
370)  myDist = myDist + 15;
                    else if (mDir == 2 & mxDist >
20)  mxDist = mxDist - 5;
                    else if (mDir == 3 & myDist >
20) myDist = myDist - 5;
            }
            if (mxDist > 360 & myDist > 360) {
                    mxDist = 380;
                    myDist = 380;
                    frenzy = null;
                    holeFlag = true;
            }
    }
    repaint();
    try {
            Thread.sleep(150);
            }
    catch(InterruptedException ie) {}
}}

public void paint(Graphics g) {

    g.setColor(Color.gray);
    g.fillOval(mxDist, myDist, 20, 20);   // Mouse

    if (holeFlag == true) {
            g.setColor(Color.white);
            g.drawString("Mouse escapes!",20, 200);
    }

    if (xDist < 25 || xDist > 375) xinc = -xinc;
    if (yDist < 25 || yDist > 375) yinc = -yinc;
    xDist = xDist + xinc;
    yDist = yDist + yinc;
    g.setColor(Color.orange);
    g.fillOval(xDist, yDist, 20, 20);     // Cat

    if (Math.abs(xDist - mxDist) < 15 &
Math.abs(yDist - myDist) < 15){
```

```
            g.drawString("Mouse caught!", 20, 200);
            caughtFlag = true;
            xinc = 0;
            yinc = 0;
            g.setColor(Color.blue);// Clear mouse
            g.fillOval(mxDist, myDist, 20, 20);
        }

        g.setColor(Color.black);
        g.fillOval(380, 380, 20, 20);              // Hole
    }}
```

The width and height of this applet are both 400.

In this chapter, there are detailed descriptions only of those routines that have features not covered in the rest of the book. To help the reader understand the listing, here is an explanation of the global variables declared on p.135.

int xDist = 30;   x-coordinate of the cat.

int yDist = 370;   y-coordinate of the cat.

int mxDist = 30;   x-coordinate of Mickey.

int myDist = 30;   y-coordinate of Mickey.

int cxDist = 0;   x-coordinate of the cursor when mouse clicked.

int cyDist = 0;   y-coordinate of the cursor when mouse clicked.

int xinc = 0;   increment of the x-coord. (positive = to the right).

int yinc = 0;   increment of the y-coord. (positive = downward).

int mDir = 0;   random direction of Mickey, value 0 to 3, 0 = right, 1 = down, 2 = left, 3 = up.

Thread frenzy = null; the thread that controls the random motion of Mickey.

boolean holeFlag = false; T = Mickey in hole.

boolean caughtFlag = false; T = Mickey caught.

The Math.abs(int) method used in Graphics() on p. 135 returns the absolute value of the integer parameter. It has a positive value, irrespective of whether the integer has a positive or negative value. In other words, it is the difference beween the coordinates, ignoring the sign. Here it is used to calculate the difference between the cat's and Mickey's coordinates. If the differences for x and y are both less than 15, the cat is considered to have caught Mickey and the game ends.

Developing Cat 'n'Mouse

With the settings as listed most players should win more often than lose. We can make the game harder by:

- Making the cat get closer to the mouse in order to catch it. Reduce the values in the if (Math.abs(xDist ... line.

- Giving Mickey more erratic motion. Increase the increments in the if (mxDist >25... block. Positive increments must be of larger absolute size than negative increments so that Mickey is biased toward the mousehole.

- Allowing Mickey a 'mouse's life' or two. He must be caught, say, two or three tmes before the cat wins.

- Add sound effects.

The game would be improved by allowing the player to select the difficulty level. Another improvement would be to use graphics images of the cat and Mickey instead of discs.

Stunt Car

This is a fast-moving game of skill for one player. It all depends on timing.

There is a road across the screen, and a little car travels at high speed along the road from left to right. When it disappears off the right side of the screen it reappears on the left.

138

You might think that it could carry on like this for ever but, unfortunately, there are three holes in the road. Each hole is large enough for the car to fall through. The only way you can stop the car from falling through is to make it jump over the holes. You do this by clicking on the "Jump" button at the top of the applet area.

Your score is displayed at the top right corner of the applet. As long as the car is actually on the road, the score increases steadily. But it stops increasing while the car is jumping.

Your task is to stay on the road as long as you can while amassing the highest possible score. Taking long jumps over the holes is safer, but you score will be lower. Short jumps give the best score but are risky. Sooner or later, you will mis-time the jump; the car falls through a hole and crashes, ending the game. Try again for a bigger score.

Fig. 23. Running in Netscape Browser, *the stunt car has successfully jumped over two holes and is heading for the third. So far, it has gained a score of 5 points. In this view, the applet is embedded in an HTML page that describes how to play.*

The game finishes when the car crashes. In *AppletViewer*, the easiest way to run the game again is to select 'Clone' from the Applet Viewer drop-down menu. You will finish up with a dozen or more clones on the screen, all now inactive because the car has crashed. Flick through them to find your best score.

In a browser, the best way to re-run the game is to return to the home page and select the game again.

This game builds on the *moveAuto* program (p. 40). You can save a lot of typing by loading the .java version of that program into your text editor and editing and expanding it. The listing of *stuntCar* is:

```java
import java.awt.*;
import java.awt.geom.*;
import java.awt.event.*;
import javax.swing.*;

public class stuntCar extends JApplet implements
ActionListener, Runnable {

    Thread mover = null;
    JButton jump;
    int xDist = -20;
    int yDist = 50;
    Image car = null;
    int inc = 3;
    int score = 0;
    boolean flagDown = true;

public void init() {
    Container road = getContentPane();
    BorderLayout jumpButton = new BorderLayout();
    road.setLayout(jumpButton);
    jump = new JButton("Jump");
    setBackground(Color.blue);
    car = getImage(getCodeBase(), "Auto1.gif");
    JPanel space = new JPanel();
    space.add(jump, BorderLayout.SOUTH);
    jump.addActionListener(this);
    road.add(space);
    setContentPane(road);
}

public void start() {
    if (mover == null) {
            mover = new Thread(this);
            mover.start();
    }}
```

```
    public void stop() {
        if (mover != null) mover = null;
            }

    public void run() {
        while (mover != null) {
                xDist = xDist + inc;
                if (xDist >= 550) {
                xDist = 0;
                }

        if (flagDown == true & ((xDist > 65 & xDist <115)
|| (xDist > 195 & xDist < 255) || (xDist > 335 & xDist <
395))) {
                inc = 0;
                yDist = 85;
                }
                if ((xDist % 10 == 0) & flagDown == true)
{
                score = score + 1;
                }
                repaint();
                try
                {Thread.sleep(60);}
                        catch(InterruptedException e){}

        }}

public void actionPerformed(ActionEvent e) {
        if (e.getActionCommand() == "Jump") {
                if (yDist == 50) {
                yDist = 40;
                flagDown = false;
                }
                else if (yDist == 40){
                yDist = 50;
                flagDown = true;
                }}
                repaint();
        }

public void paint(Graphics g) {
        Graphics2D g2D = (Graphics2D)g;
        jump.setBackground(Color.orange);
        jump.setForeground(Color.cyan);
        g2D.setColor(Color.gray);

        for (int j = 0; j < 500; j = j + 140) {
        Rectangle2D.Float potholed = new Rectan-
gle2D.Float(j, 72F, 80F, 25F);
        g2D.fill(potholed);
        }
```

```
g2D.setColor(Color.blue);
      Rectangle2D.Float blankit =
new Rectangle2D.Float(xDist - 5, 40F, 50F, 32F);
      g2D.fill(blankit);
      if (xDist % 10 == 0)  {
      Rectangle2D.Float blankscore =
new Rectangle2D.Float(400F, 20F, 90F, 20F);
      g2D.fill(blankscore);
      }
      g2D.drawImage(car, xDist, yDist, this);
      g2D.setColor(Color.white);
      g2D.drawString("Score:", 400, 20);
}}
```

The width of this applet is 500 and the height is 100.

The listing is not much longer than *moveAuto*, but the few additions have converted it from a demonstration of animation to become a fast-moving game.

The variable declarations are:

Thread mover	Moves the car.
JButton	The jump button.
int xDist	x-coordinate of the car.
int yDist	y-coordinate of the car.
Image car	Image of the car.
int inc	Increments the x-coordinate.
int score	Player's score.
boolean flagDown	T = car down on road.

The image Auto1.gif is 47 pixels wide and 22 pixels high; you may need to change a few xDist and yDist values if your image is a different size.

The actionPerformed() method of *moveAuto* has been altered to handle the new button function. This has a toggle action, putting the car down if it is up, or up if it is down. At the same time, the value of flagDown (true or false) is set accordingly.

142

Developing the *stuntCar* program

There are several ways in which you can improve on the basic program:

Speed: You may find that it is too easy to avoid the holes. The speed of the car can be increased by editing the value of `inc` to 4 or 5. Do this where `inc` is first declared. Or you could try reducing the length of the `sleep` in the `run()` method. An even better idea is to create a routine by which the difficulty level (that is, `inc` or the length of `sleep`) can be set by clicking on a button.

Playing again: Devise a routine for beginning the game again after the car has crashed. You could also arrange for your best score of the session to be displayed, as well as the score for the current run.

Animation: Introduce a sequence of images so that the car appears to disintegrate when it crashes.

Sound effects: Add the sound of a fast-moving car when it is on the road, a jet plane when the car is jumping, and an ear-splitting crash at the end.

Sniper

This is a shoot 'em up game in which quick reactions and accurate aim are the prime requirements. The scenario is that a gang of ten terrorists have occupied a building and your task, as a goodie, is to force them to surrender. The terrorists are each equipped with a rifle and are trained snipers. Although you are well protected in an armoured vehicle, each sniper has a 1 in 20 chance of hitting you and making you retire from the game.

You have a machine gun and are an excellent shot with this. But you have a limited suppy of ammunition — only enough for 20 bursts of fire. Once each terrorist is hit they do not fire again. The remainder of the gang surrender when there are only three of them left. You win if you can hit seven before a lucky terrorist shot hits you.

In play, the scene of action is a photograph or drawing of the occupied building. Ours is a photograph of an up-market three-storey apartment block, It has plenty of cover for the terrorists with lots of windows, doorways and balconies from which the gang can open fire. The photograph is the full size of the applet. Instead of a photograph you could use a drawing.

When the program is run, the snipers are positioned at ten randomly chosen locations. This means that you are very unlikely to get the same configuration twice in different sessions. The snipers fire at random too, so you never know where the next bullet will come from.

You control your machine gun with the mouse. The cursor shows where you are aiming. To open the game, you click the button and hear a burst of machine-gun fire.

There is a delay while the snipers take aim. The length of the delay is set at random so you are kept in suspense, waiting to be shot at. For until you have located a sniper it is a waste of your limited ammunition to fire indiscriminately.

When a sniper fires, you hear the sound of a rifle shot and a small yellow disc appears briefly at the sniper's location. Move the cursor to that point as quickly and accurately as you can and click the button. If you are succesful the message "Sniper hit" appears briefly on the screen.

The skirmish continues, with the snipers firing and you trying to fire back. The game ends, with you as winner, when there are only three snipers surviving. The game ends with the snipers as winners, if one of the snipers hits you, or if you run out of ammunition.

In *Applet Viewer*, the easiest way to run the game again is to select 'Clone' from the *Applet Viewer* drop-down menu. You will finish up with a dozen or more clones on the screen, all now inactive because of one of the endings described above. Flick through them to find which side won most often. In a browser, the best way to re-run the game is to return to the home page and select the game again.

The first thing you need for building this program is an image of an apartment block. Or it might be anything else — from an ancient castle to a city office-block to a woodland glade. Preferably the photo should be a landscape shape. The greater the width of the picture the more widely the player has to scan to watch for the rifle flashes. Then the cursor may have to be swept from one side of the screen to the other to return fire. The image file should be in .gif or .jpg format and saved in the same folder as the .class file of the game.

Sound effects heighten the excitement of the game. One is a short audio clip of a single rifle shot. The other is a short burst of machine-gun fire. There are several suitable clips on the Internet (p. 38) but choose short ones. Otherwise they play for too long and delay the start of the next shot. If necessary, use an audio utility such as *Nero Wave Editor* to cut the clip short, cutting out any initial quiet period.

The listing is:

```java
import java.awt.*;
import java.awt.geom.*;
import java.awt.event.*;
import javax.swing.*;
import java.net.*;
import java.applet.*;

public class sniper extends JApplet implements
Runnable, MouseListener {

Image flats;
Thread snipers = null;
Thread goodie = null;
float sxDist = 0;
float syDist = 0;
float[] enemyx = new float[9];
float[] enemyy = new float[9];
boolean[] enemyFlag = new boolean[9];
int active;
int time;
int mxDist = 0;
int myDist = 0;
int snipersHit = 0;
int mgBursts = 0;
int fireHit = 0;
```

```
AudioClip soundfx1;
AudioClip soundfx2;

boolean startFlag = false;
boolean goodieFlag  = false;
boolean hitFlag = false;
boolean skirmishFlag = false;
boolean sniperFlag = false;
boolean goodieHitFlag = false;
boolean mgFireFlag = false;
Font large;

public void init() {

    Container base = getContentPane();
    JPanel scene = new JPanel();
    scene.addMouseListener(this);
    base.add(scene);
    setContentPane(base);
    setBackground(Color.green);
    flats = getImage(getCodeBase(),"APARTMEN.gif");
    soundfx1 =
getAudioClip(getCodeBase(),"rifle1.wav");
    soundfx2 =
getAudioClip(getCodeBase(),"mgun.wav");
}

public void start() {
    if (snipers == null) snipers = new Thread(this);
            snipers.start();
    if (goodie == null) goodie = new Thread(this);
            goodie.start();
}

public void stop() {
    if (snipers != null) snipers = null;
    if (goodie != null) goodie = null;
}

public void run() {

// SNIPERS LOOP

    while (snipers == Thread.currentThread() ) {

// Waiting phase

            while (startFlag == true) {
```

146

```
// Setup phase

     if (skirmishFlag == false) {
          for (int j = 0; j < 9;j = j + 1){
                    enemyx[j] = (float)(Math.random()
* 627);
                    enemyFlag[j] = true;
          }


          for (int j = 0; j < 9;j = j + 1)
enemyy[j] = (float)(Math.random() * 196);
          snipersHit = 0; mgBursts = 0; hitFlag =
false; goodieHitFlag = false;
          skirmishFlag = true; sniperFlag = false;
mgFireFlag = false;
}

// Varying delay phase
          time = (int)(Math.random() * 4500);
          try {
          Thread.sleep(1000 + time);
          }
          catch(InterruptedException e) {}

// Sniper fire phase
          sniperFlag = false;
          active = (int)(Math.random() * 9);
          if (enemyFlag[active] == true) {
                    sxDist = enemyx[active];
                    syDist = enemyy[active];
                    sniperFlag = true;
                    repaint();
                    soundfx1.play();
          }
          fireHit = (int)(Math.random() * 21);
          goodieHitFlag = false;
          if (fireHit > 19) {
                    goodieHitFlag = true;
                    repaint();
          }
}}

// goodie LOOP
     while (goodie == Thread.currentThread() ) {

// Waiting phase
     while (startFlag == true) {

// Setup phase
     if (goodieFlag == false) {
          snipersHit = 0; mgBursts = 0; hitFlag =
false;
```

147

```
                    sniperFlag = false; mgFireFlag = false;
goodieFlag = true;
      }

// Goodie fire phase
      if (mgFireFlag == true) {
            mgFireFlag = false;
            mgBursts = mgBursts + 1;
      if    (Math.abs(mxDist  -   sxDist)  <   100   &
Math.abs(myDist - syDist) < 100){
            hitFlag = true;
            repaint();
            }
      }
}}}

public void mousePressed(MouseEvent mp) {

      soundfx2.play();
      mxDist = mp.getX();
      myDist = mp.getY();
      mgFireFlag = true;
      startFlag = true;
}

public void mouseReleased(MouseEvent e) { }
public void mouseClicked(MouseEvent e) { }
public void mouseEntered(MouseEvent e) { }
public void mouseExited(MouseEvent e) { }

public void paint(Graphics g)  {

      Graphics2D g2D = (Graphics2D)g;
      g2D.drawImage(flats, 0, 0, this);

      if (sniperFlag == true) {
            g2D.setColor(Color.yellow);
            Ellipse2D.Float    rifle    =    new    El-
lipse2D.Float(sxDist, syDist, 10F, 10F);
            g2D.fill(rifle);
            try {
            Thread.sleep(1000);
            }
            catch(InterruptedException ie) { }
            g2D.drawImage(flats, 0, 0, this);
            }
      Font  large  =  new Font("SansSerif",  Font.BOLD,
40);
      g2D.setFont(large);
      g2D.setColor(Color.red);

// Display phase
      if (hitFlag == true) {
```

```
                hitFlag = false;
                enemyFlag[active] = false;
                g2D.drawString("Sniper hit", 30, 40);
                snipersHit = snipersHit + 1;
                }

        if (snipersHit > 6) {
                g2D.drawString("Snipers surrender", 30,
   80);
                startFlag = false;
                goodieFlag = false;
                skirmishFlag = false;
        }
        if (goodieHitFlag == true) {
                g2D.drawString("Badly hit - retire", 30,
   120);
                startFlag = false;
                goodieFlag = false;
                skirmishFlag = false;
        }
        if (mgBursts > 20){
                g2D.drawString("No ammo - retire!", 30,
   160);
                startFlag = false;
                goodieFlag = false;
                skirmishFlag = false;
        }

}}
```

To fit the image, the width of this applet is 627 and the height is 196.
Alter these dimensions to fit your photo.

The program is based in two loops, in the run() method. They are
controlled by two threads, snipers and goodies. The sniper loop
has four phases: waiting (for the player to start the game), setup, delay
of varying length, sniper fire. The goodies loop has three phases:
waiting, setup, goodie fire. These loops take effect in the display phase,
which is in the paint() method.

The functions of most of the global variables are obvious from their
names. The pair named enemyx[] and enemyy[] are arrays
holding the ten x-coordinates and ten y-coordinates of the snipers.
These are allocated randomly selected values within the range of
coordinates available in the image units. This is done during the setup
phase of the snipers loop.

149

There is a third 10-cell array, enemyFlag[] which holds Boolean variables. These are set to true when the coordinates are selected in the other two arrays. In the sniper fire phase the randomly chosen sniper can fire only if this flag is true.

In the display phase, the enemyFlag[] value is set to false if the sniper is hit. For the rest of the game, that sniper is unable to fire, thus increasing the player's chance of survival.

The result of having two threads

The loops run by sniper and goodie threads operate independently. They start together after the initial waiting phase but, from then on the loops take different and unpredictable times to run, so they are entirely unsynchronised. This is intended to simulate the behaviour of two opposing forces under battle conditions. Each side attacks the other as fast and effectively as it can manage, hoping to be the first to get the upper hand.

As a result of this independent activity, the relative timing of the two loops is unpredictable. The outcome of an exchange of fire does not always follow the strict pattern of aim, fire, hit or miss, display message. In battle conditions, the situation is changing so rapidly that conditions change. Orders may be ignored and messages may fail to arrive. In this way, the sniper game illustrates the meaning of the term 'Fog of War', an expression well known to wargamers.

Developing the game

The values in the listing produce a game that is reasonably easy to win.

There are several ways of making it harder:

- Increase the number of snipers by increasing the size of the arrays.
- Increase the risk of the player being hit by decreasing the threshold level of fireHit in the sniper fire phase.

- Decrease the chance of a goodie hit by reducing the thresholds in the if (Math.abs(... conditionals in the goodies fire phase.
- Increase the rate of sniper fire by reducing the sleep parameters in the varying delay phase.

The first and major section of this Part is a digest or summary of all you need to know to start writing applets.

Java digest

The digest does not include the core elements of *Java* such as data types and operators, or programming structures such as loops. Refer to a general book on *Java* for these.

Names or values to be chosen and inserted by the user are <u>underlined</u>. Coordinates of points are reckoned from the **top** left corner of a window, in pixels.

The topics explained in this part are listed below. Many of them are illustrated by a 'Digest' program which you can type in and run.

1 Applet methods

A typical applet program comprises five methods, called in this order, immediately after the class variables (if any) have been declared:

- *init()* Initialises the applet. The method is called (either by listing a call or automatically) when the applet is first run. It is not called again in the same session.
- *start()* This starts the applet running, and is called every time the applet is run or its page is reloaded.
- *paint()* This method is called to place the defined text and images on the screen. The method *repaint()* is used in the program to redraw the applet after changes have been made in the material to be displayed. The screen is repainted automatically after it has been partly or totally overwritten by other windows that are subsequently removed to reveal the applet again.

- *stop()* Stops the applet from running when the browser displays a different *HTML* page. The applet begins running again (from the *start()* method) if the user returns to the page.

- *destroy()* The applet is cleared from memory.

The **run()** method is used in applets to oversee the action of one or more threads (p. 183). Applets do not have a **main()** method.

2 Imported packages

Java 1 applets: `import java.applet.*;` and `import java.awt.*;`
Java 2 applets (advanced graphics etc): `import javax.swing.*;`
For 2D graphics: `import java.awt.geom.*;`
For handling events in Java 2: `import java.awt.event.*;`
For playing sounds: `import java.net.*;` and
`import java.applet.*;`

3 Class declaration

Java 1 applets:
`public class appletClassName extends Applet {}`

Java 2 applets, using swing:
`public class appletClassName extends JApplet {}`

When ActionListener is used:
`public class appletClassName extends JApplet implements ActionListener {}`

MouseListener requires the equivalent declaration.

When a thread is used:
`public class appletClassName extends JApplet implements Runnable { } ;`

When there are two or more implementations, for example:

```
public class appletClassName extends JApplet
implements MouseListener, Runnable {
```

4 Colours

Applets use 13 pre-defined colours:

black, darkGray, gray, lightGray, pink, red, orange, yellow, green, cyan, blue, magenta, white.

Some of the applet colours match the *HTML* colours.

Alternatively, a colour can be defined as an instance, like this:

```
Color colourName =
   new Color(int,
      int, int);
```

The three 'ints' represent the proportions of red, green and blue, and values range from zero (dark) to 255 (bright). Coded colours are particularly useful for obtaining very light and very dark colours.

HTML

There are 16 pre-defined colours:

black, gray (Note the spelling), silver (a light grey), red, maroon, purple, fuchsia (a light purple), lime (a light green), yellow, olive, green, blue, navy, teal (a darkish greeny-blue), aqua (cyan), and white.

HTML

Coded colours are defined in an HTML listing like this:

BGCOLOR="#RRGGBB"

The code represents three two-digit hex values representing the proportions of red, green and blue.

5 Setting colours

The background of the default applet window is white.

In init() use:

```
setBackground(Color.colourName);
setForeground(Color.colourName);
```

In paint(Graphics g) use:

```
g.setColor(Color.colourName);
```

This sets the current drawing colour for text and graphics.

When using Graphics2D, first cast the Graphics object g (by convention) to form a Graphics2D object, g2D:

```
Graphics2D g2D = (Graphics2D)g;
```

Then set the current drawing colour:

```
g2D.setColor(Color.colourName);
```

The colour name can be either pre-defined or user-defined by code.

Fig. 24 . First view of Digest1, before editing.

Digest1 is a workbench for colours, fonts and text:

```java
import java.awt.*;
import javax.swing.*;

/*
<APPLET CODE=digest1 WIDTH=300 HEIGHT=200>
</APPLET>
*/

public class digest1 extends JApplet {

//Workbench for colours, fonts and text.

     Color sage;
     Font demoFont;

public void init() {

     Color sage = new Color(150, 150, 50);
     setBackground(Color.yellow);
     }

public void paint (Graphics g) {
     Graphics2D g2D = (Graphics2D)g;

     g2D.setColor(sage);
     Font demoFont = new Font("Mistral", Font.PLAIN,
24);
     g2D.setFont(demoFont);
     String sampleText = "This is in the chosen
font";
     g2D.drawString(sampleText, 20, 40);
     g2D.drawString("or use the actual string.", 20,
60);
     }
}
```

Fig. 24 (opposite) shows the demonstration message. Try editing the listing to change colours, font, point size, and the messages.

Design some new colours and use them for the background and the text.

6 Fonts

Default font is a san-serif font similar to Arial.

Define a custom font by:

```
Font  fontName  =  new  Font("actualName",  int,
int);
```

An example of `actualName` is "CourierNew". First int is style in which 0 = regular, 1 = bold, 2 = italic, 3 = bold italic. Second int is size in points. In Graphics2D, instead of the first int, we can use a constant: PLAIN, BOLD, or ITALIC.

Having defined the font, set it as the current font with:

```
g2D.setFont(fontName)
```

7 Text strings

Declare as:

```
String    nameOf String;
```

Is global if declared immediately after class declaration. May be given a value then or later.

In paint() use:

```
        g.drawString(nameOfString, int, int);
```

This is possibly preceded by setting colour and/or font. The two ints are the x- and y-coordinates of the start of the string. Alternatively, use:

```
        g.drawString("actualString", int, int);
```

In Graphics2D, replace g with g2D.

8 Lines

(a) For a simple line 1 pixel wide, default colour black or the current drawing colour, use in paint():

```
g.drawLine(int, int, int, int);
```

The first two ints are x- and y-coordinates of the beginning of the line; the second two ints are the coordinates of the other end.

(b) For wider or more elaborate lines use, the Graphics2D method based on BasicStroke(), in the four stages below.

(i) Declare the line using:

```
BasicStroke lineName = new BasicStroke(float);
```

The float defines line width in pixels.

(ii) Set the current line width with:

```
g2D.setStroke(lineName);
```

(iii) Define an instance of the line with:

```
Line2D.Float instanceName = new
Line2D.Float(float, float, float, float);
```

The four floats are the coordinates of the ends of the line. It is safer to append 'F' to each if they are entered as integers.

(iv) Draw the line with:

```
g2D.draw(instanceName);
```

Variations in the line are programmed by two optional parameters at stage (iii) above:

float	line width in pixels (already quoted above)
int	BasicStroke.CAP_BUTT, or BasicStroke.CAP_ROUND, or BasicStroke.CAP.SQUARE These define the shape of the ends of the line.
int	BasicStroke.JOIN_BEVEL, or BasicStroke.JOIN_MITER, or BasicStroke.JOIN_ROUND. These define the join between lines, but only in the GeneralPath() method (see next). BasicStroke() ignores joins, so use the default JOIN_BEVEL as the third parameter.

Three more optional parameters in BasicStroke() are:

    int   mitre limit, which cuts short any long 'points' if the miter joins lines at acute angles. Use 0 if there are no miter joins.

    new float[ ]   An array to hold the pattern of a dashed line, The values listed in the square brackets may be a single integer (dashes and gaps of equal length, in pixels), a pair of ints (dash, gap) or a sequence of ints (dash, gap, alternately).

    int   The dash phase, the starting point of the first dash in the series, reckoned in pixels from the beginning of the series. Use 0 if the line begins at the start of the series.

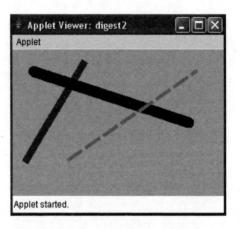

Fig. 25. The aim of these 'Digest' programs is to give the reader a set of examples of Java *commands and what they do. There is scope for editing the program to explore how to make best use of them.*
In Digest2 *(above), we look at the essential topic of drawing lines with BasicStroke().*

Digest2 is a program for trying out the many ways of drawing lines, using BasicStroke().

```
import java.awt.*;
import java.awt.geom.*;
import javax.swing.*;

/*
<APPLET CODE=digest2 WIDTH=300 HEIGHT=200>
</APPLET>
*/

public class digest2 extends JApplet {

//Workbench for lines using BasicStroke().

public void init(){

    setBackground(Color.lightGray);

    }

public void paint (Graphics g) {
    Graphics2D g2D = (Graphics2D)g;

    g2D.setColor(Color.red);
    BasicStroke wideLine = new BasicStroke(10F);
    g2D.setStroke(wideLine);
    Line2D.Float demoLine1 = new Line2D.Float(20F,
150F, 100F, 20F);
    g2D.draw(demoLine1);

    g2D.setColor(Color.blue);
    BasicStroke roundends = new BasicStroke(15F,
 BasicStroke.CAP_ROUND, BasicStroke.JOIN_BEVEL);
    g2D.setStroke(roundends);
    Line2D.Float demoLine2 = new Line2D.Float(30F,
30F, 250F, 100F);
    g2D.draw(demoLine2);

    g2D.setColor(Color.green);
    BasicStroke dashes = new BasicStroke(5F,
 BasicStroke.CAP_SQUARE,
 BasicStroke.JOIN_BEVEL, 0, new float[] {20, 10},
0);
    g2D.setStroke(dashes);
    Line2D.Float demoLine3 = new Line2D.Float(80F,
150F, 260F, 30F);
    g2D.draw(demoLine3);

  }}
```

(c) Use the GeneralPath() swing method for drawing polygons and multisegmented lines. The procedure is:

(i) Set the colour as usual, using the setColor() method.

(ii) Declare:

```
GeneralPath(pathName);
```

(iii) Define the line using the BasicStroke() method as described in paragraph (a) on pp.158-159.

(iv) Create an instance of GeneralPath, using:

```
pathName = new GeneralPath();
```

(v) Define starting point with:

```
pathName.moveTo(float, float);
```

(vi) Use a series of lineTo() commands, with float cordinates to draw the line to the next point.

(vii) If the path is to be closed (a polygon), use:

```
pathName.closePath();
```

This has no argument.

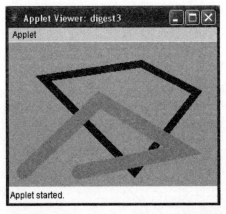

Fig. 26. A closed path (dark) and an open path (light), drawn by Digest3. The open path has round ends and mitre joins.

162

Digest3 illustrates another line-drawing method.

```java
import java.awt.*;
import java.awt.geom.*;
import javax.swing.*;

/*
<APPLET CODE=digest3 WIDTH=300 HEIGHT=200>
</APPLET>
*/

public class digest3 extends JApplet {

//Workbench for lines using GeneralPath().

public void init() {

    setBackground(Color.pink);

    }

public void paint (Graphics g) {
    Graphics2D g2D = (Graphics2D)g;

    g2D.setColor(Color.blue);
    GeneralPath bluePath;
    BasicStroke wideLine = new BasicStroke(10F);
    g2D.setStroke(wideLine);
    bluePath = new GeneralPath();
    bluePath.moveTo(50, 50);
    bluePath.lineTo(180, 180);
    bluePath.lineTo(270, 70);
    bluePath.lineTo(190, 30);
    bluePath.closePath(); //Comment this out to get
open path.
    g2D.draw(bluePath);

g2D.setColor(Color.cyan);
    GeneralPath cyanPath;
    BasicStroke miterLine = new BasicStroke(20F,
BasicStroke.CAP_ROUND,
BasicStroke.JOIN_MITER,5F);
    g2D.setStroke(miterLine);
    cyanPath = new GeneralPath();
    cyanPath.moveTo(20, 180);
    cyanPath.lineTo(130, 80);
    cyanPath.lineTo(250, 150);
    cyanPath.lineTo(100, 180);
    g2D.draw(cyanPath);

 }}
```

163

9 Rectangles and ellipses

In `paint(Graphics g)`, basic rectangles (including squares) are drawn with lines only 1 pixel wide.

For an open rectangle, use:

```
g.drawRect(int, int, int, int);
```

First two ints are x- and y-coordinates of the top left corner. The third int is the width, and the fourth is the height.

For a filled rectangle, use:

```
g.fillRect (int, int, int, int);
```

Ints are as above.

For an open rectangle with rounded corners, use:

```
g.drawRoundRect(int, int, int, int, int, int);
```

The fifth and sixth ints set the diameters of the corners in the x- and y-directions.

For a filled rectangle with rounded corners, use:

```
g.fillRoundRect(int, int, int, int, int, int);
```

For Graphics2D rectangles, first declare an instance:

```
Rectangle2D.Float rectangleName =
new Rectangle2D.Float(float, float, float,
float);
```

Ints defned as above. Rectangles with rounded corners are obtained similarly by using `RoundRectangle2D.Float()`.

Then, draw the rectangle by:

```
g2D.draw(rectangleName);
```

or fill the rectangle by:

```
g2D.fill(rectangleName);
```

An ellipse is drawn inside an imaginary rectangle, defined as above. The equivalent methods are:

```
g.drawOval(int, int, int,int);
g.fillOval(int, int, int, int);
Ellipse2D.Float.ellipseName =
 new Ellipse2D.Float(float, float,
 float, float);
g2Ddraw(ellipseName);
g2Dfill(ellipseName);
```

Digest4 displays an open blue rectangle, an open red rectangle with rounded corners, both drawn with the default line 1 pixel wide. It displays a green filled rectangle and then an open white ellipse. The ellipse shows how these 2D figures can be drawn with lines previously defined with BasicStroke().

```
import java.awt.*;
import java.awt.geom.*;
import javax.swing.*;

/*
<APPLET CODE=digest4 WIDTH=300 HEIGHT=200>
</APPLET>
*/

public class digest4 extends JApplet {

//Workbench for Graphics2D rectangles and ellipses.

public void init() {

    setBackground(Color.orange);
    }

public void paint (Graphics g) {
    Graphics2D g2D = (Graphics2D)g;

    g2D.setColor(Color.blue);
    Rectangle2D.Float blueRect = new
Rectangle2D.Float(40F, 20F, 120F, 60F);
    g2D.draw(blueRect);
```

Continued overleaf

```
        g2D.setColor(Color.red);
        Rectangle2D.Float redRect = new
   Rectangle2D.Float(200F, 30F, 50F, 160F);
        g2D.fill(redRect);

        g2D.setColor(Color.green);
        RoundRectangle2D.Float greenRect = new
   RoundRectangle2D.Float(20F, 120F, 100F, 60F, 5F,
   10F);
        g2D.draw(greenRect);

        g2D.setColor(Color.white);
        BasicStroke boldLine = new BasicStroke(8);
        g2D.setStroke(boldLine);
        Ellipse2D.Float whiteElps = new
   Ellipse2D.Float(60F, 60F, 200F, 100F);
        g2D.draw(whiteElps);

}}
```

10 Arcs

There are three types of arc: open, pie and chord. An arc is defined by seven parameters, as if it is part of an ellipse enclosed in an imaginary rectangle:

float   x-coordinate of top left corner of rectangle.

float   y-coordinate of top left corner of rectangle.

float   width of rectangle.

float   height of rectangle.

float   start point, reckoned in degrees anticlockwise from 3 o'clock.

float   angle subtended by the arc, in degrees.

type   either OPEN, PIE, or CHORD.

See the listing opposite for the syntax of the definition, and Fig. 27 (p. 168) for a picture of the results.

Digest5, an assortment of arcs, drawn with lines defined by BasicStroke(). The result of running this program is shown overleaf, in Fig. 27.

```
import java.awt.*;
import java.awt.geom.*;
import javax.swing.*;

/*
<APPLET CODE=digest5 WIDTH=300 HEIGHT=200>
</APPLET>
*/

public class digest5 extends JApplet {

//Workbench for Graphics2D arcs.

public void init() {

    setBackground(Color.magenta);
    }

public void paint (Graphics g) {
    Graphics2D g2D = (Graphics2D)g;

    BasicStroke boldLine = new BasicStroke(8);
    g2D.setStroke(boldLine);

    g2D.setColor(Color.blue);
    Arc2D.Float blueOpen = new Arc2D.Float(40F,
20F, 120F, 120F, 0F, 120F, Arc2D.Float.OPEN);
    g2D.draw(blueOpen);

    g2D.setColor(Color.cyan);
    Arc2D.Float cyanPie = new Arc2D.Float(40F, 80F,
 200F, 90F, 180F, 90F, Arc2D.Float.PIE);
    g2D.fill(cyanPie);

    g2D.setColor(Color.yellow);
    Arc2D.Float yellowChord = new Arc2D.Float(150F,
50F, 80F, 100F, 315F, 90F, Arc2D.Float.CHORD);
    g2D.draw(yellowChord);

}}
```

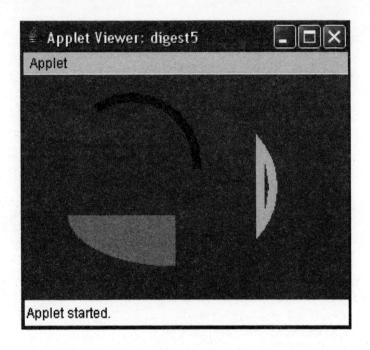

Fig. 27. Three types of arc: open (top left), pie (lower left), and chord (right).

11 Polygons

The simplest technique is to set up two integer arrays, xDist[ ] and yDist[ ] to hold the coordinates of the corners. Declare an int variable sides for the number of sides of the polygon. Then use:

```
g.drawPolygon(xDist, yDist, sides); or
 g.fillPolygon(xDist, yDist, sides);
```

For a polygon drawn in wider lines, or other advanced features, create a closed GeneralPath object, as in Fig. 26.

168

12 Images

Save the image as a .gif or .jpg file in the same folder as the program, under <u>fileName</u>.gif or <u>fileName.</u>.jpg. In the class listing, declare the image by Image <u>imageName</u>;. In the init() method define:

```
imageName = getImage(getCodeBase(),
"fileName.gif");.
```

In the paint() method, use the statement g.drawImage(<u>imageName, int, int,</u> this);. The ints are the coordinates of the top left corner.

Digest6 displays images. Captions can be added, either over or beside the image, as shown below and overleaf.

```
import java.awt.*;
import java.awt.geom.*;
import javax.swing.*;

/*
<APPLET CODE=digest6 WIDTH=400 HEIGHT=400>
</APPLET>
*/

public class digest6 extends JApplet {

//Workbench for Graphics2D arcs.

Image apple;

Font photoText = new Font("Rockwell", Font.PLAIN,
30);

public void init() {
    apple = getImage(getCodeBase(), "APPLE.jpg");
    setBackground(Color.magenta);
    }

public void paint (Graphics g) {
    Graphics2D g2D = (Graphics2D)g;

    g2D.drawImage(apple, 10, 10, this);
    g2D.setColor(Color.white);
    g2D.setFont(photoText);
```

```
String caption1 = "Guess what! - this is an";
String caption2 = "apple(t).";
g2D.drawString(caption1, 25, 335);
g2D.drawString(caption2, 25, 365);
```

}}

Fig. 28. Photographic images and
drawings can be displayed in an
applet in full colour.

13 Sounds, the use of flags, and exception handling

In Digests 7 and 7A, the sounds are triggered by events. Programming events is explained on p. 175 and in Section 15, p. 178. The *digest7* program listed opposite and on pp. 172-173, shows how to handle sound files. Sounds — music or sound effects — are programmed in three steps.

If possible, save the audio clip in the same folder as the .class file. The steps are very similar to those for loading and displaying images (p. 169).

The programming is as follows:

i) Declare the description you will give to the AudioClip object, the sound track that is to be played:

```
AudioClip   trackDescription;
```

(ii) In init() or where the sound is to be played (as in the actionPerformed() method in this example), create the new AudioClip object:

```
trackDescription =
getAudioClip(getCodeBase(),"URLOfTheFile");
```

If the file is in the same folder as the program, the URL of the file is simply the file name, as on p. 172. If you are working on line and the sound file is on a different web site, give the full URL of the site plus the file name.

(iii) Play the track; for a single playing, use:

```
trackDescription.play();
```

For continuous play, use:

```
trackDescription.loop();
```

To end the loop use:

```
trackDescription.stop();
```

Digest7 plays sounds and shows how to program Action Events.

For **sound only:** omit lines that are commented out with //, and omit the block from /* to */ on p. 173.

For **sound and graphics:** type the whole listing, leaving out the //, /* and */ symbols on the left, except those commenting out the HTML code.

171

```
import java.awt.*;
import java.awt.geom.*;
import java.awt.event.*;
import javax.swing.*;
import java.applet.*;
import java.net.*;

/*
<APPLET CODE=digest7 WIDTH=400 HEIGHT=200>
</APPLET>
*/

public class digest7 extends JApplet implements
ActionListener {

    JButton cat;
    JButton dog;
    AudioClip soundfx;
//  Boolean flagcat = false;
//  Boolean flagdog = false;

public void init() {

    Container pickpet = getContentPane();
    FlowLayout control = new FlowLayout();
    pickpet.setLayout(control);
    cat = new JButton("Cat");
    dog = new JButton("Dog");
    cat.addActionListener(this);
    dog.addActionListener(this);
    pickpet.add(cat);
    pickpet.add(dog);
    setBackground(Color.yellow);
    setContentPane(pickpet);
    }

public void actionPerformed (ActionEvent e) {

    Object source = e.getSource();
    if (source == cat){
//  flagcat = true;
    soundfx      =      getAudioClip(getCodeBase(),
"MEOW.wav");
    soundfx.play();
    }
    else if (source == dog){
//  flagdog = true;
    soundfx      =      getAudioClip(getCodeBase(),
"BIG_DOG_.wav");
    soundfx.play();
    }
//  repaint();
    }
```

```
public void paint (Graphics g) {
    Graphics2D g2D = (Graphics2D)g;

    cat.setBackground(Color.red);
    cat.setForeground(Color.green);
    dog.setBackground(Color.green);
    dog.setForeground(Color.red);
    g2D.setColor(Color.yellow);
    Rectangle2D.Float blankit = new
 Rectangle2D.Float(140F, 40F, 130F, 120F);
    g2D.fill(blankit);
/*  g2D.setColor(Color.black);
    if (flagcat == true) {
    flagcat = false;
    g2D.drawString("Poor Pussy!",150, 50);
    Image pet = getImage(getCodeBase(),
"catmeow.gif");
    g2D.drawImage(pet, 150, 60, this);
    }
    if (flagdog == true) {
    flagdog = false;
    g2D.drawString("Down! Fido, Down!",150, 50);
    Image pet = getImage(getCodeBase(),
"dogbark.gif");
    g2D.drawImage(pet, 150, 60, this);
    }                *//
}}
```

Fig. 29. Digest7 running on-line in an HTML page, using
Netscape Browser 8. *The "Dog" button has just been pressed,*
and the barking sound effect is playing.

173

In digest7, stage (i) comes just after the class declaration. Stages (ii) and (iii) are present twice each in the `actionPerformed()` method.

Flags

This program has flag variables to control its actions. A flag may take one of two states, depending on whether or not a particular event has occurred. A flag variable may conveniently be a Boolean.

This program has two flags: `flagcat` and `flagdog`, which are `true` when the respective button has been clicked on recently, but are otherwise `false`. They are declared as `false` to begin with, but the appropriate one is made true (in the `actionPerformed()` method) when a button is clicked on. The state of the flags is used in the `paint()` method to display either the cat image or the dog image, or to simply blank out the existing image.

Note that immediately the flag has been read as `true` in the conditional `if ()` statement, it is cleared to `false`, ready to register the next click.

Handling exceptions

The version of *Digest7* listed on pp. 172-173 is intended for viewing off-line in a browser or in applet viewer. However, if it is intended to be downloaded from a web site we need to take precautions against something going wrong with the file transfer from the server, or perhaps because the web address is not exactly correct.

If such exceptions occur the program will crash, but if the exceptions are properly dealt with the program can continue running. Of course, no image will appear or no sound effect be heard, but the program continus without them.

For on-line use, add exception handling routines in both the `actionPerformed()` and `paint()` methods.

174

We use the try{} command around the statements concerned with downloading the sound and graphics files. The format is:

```
try {
<Downloading statement>
}
```

This block is followed by:

```
catch(MalformedURLException error) {}
```

The empty curly brackets indicate that no action is to be taken if such an exception occurs. The program will keep on running, but without the sound or graphics.

In some cases you may want to take a positive action as a result of the exception. For example to display a message reporting the failure to download. The statement for such actions is then included within the curly brackets.

Mouse events

In *digest7A* the action is triggered by moving the mouse over a button, instead of clicking on it. The listing is as *digest7*, except for the following changes:

(i) In the class declaration, replace the term ActionListener by MouseListener.

(ii) Change `actionPerformed(ActionEvent e)` to `mouseEntered(MouseEvent e)`. The contents of the method remain unchanged.

(iii) After the mouseEntered() method, add empty methods for the unused mouse event methods:

```
public void mousePressed(MouseEvent e) {}
public void mouseReleased(MouseEvent e) {}
public void mouseClicked(MouseEvent e) {}
public void mouseExited(MouseEvent e) {}
```

Note that all mouse event methods must be included in the listing, whether or not they are actually used.

14 Buttons

Buttons can be defined with text on them or with images, using the JButton() methods:

```
JButton buttonName = new JButton("text");
```
or
```
   ImageIcon imageName = new
   ImageIcon("fileName");
   JButton buttonName = new JButton(imageName);
```

or with both parameters, text followed by imageName.

Then add the button to the event listener and to the container before setting the content pane. By default, the buttons appear as raised convex rectangles in shades of grey. The colour of the button and text can be set as in the listings, but then the button is displayed as a flat rectangle (example, see Fig. 29, p. 173).

When the response text changes in *Digest8*, a rectangle (with the same colour as the background) is drawn to delete the old text.

Many of the button methods are also available in *Java 1*. We use these in digest8 to demonstrate what can be done with the earlier versions.

Here is the *Java 1* listing:

```
import java.awt.*;
import java.applet.*;

public class digest8 extends Applet {

//Workbench for interface buttons (Java 1 version).

     String response;
     Button clickOnMe = new Button("Click on me");
     Button orMe = new Button("... or me ...");
     Button orPossiblyMe = new Button("or possibly
me");
```

```
public void init() {

     FlowLayout dexter = new FlowLay-
out(FlowLayout.RIGHT);
     setLayout(dexter);
     clickOnMe.setBackground(Color.blue);
     clickOnMe.setForeground(Color.yellow);
     add(clickOnMe);
     orMe.setBackground(Color.red);
     orMe.setForeground(Color.black);
     add(orMe);
     orPossiblyMe.setBackground(Color.yellow);
     orPossiblyMe.setForeground(Color.red);
     add(orPossiblyMe);
     setBackground(Color.cyan);
}

public boolean action(Event e, Object ob) {

     if (e.target == clickOnMe) {
     response = "Blue button";}
     if (e.target == orMe){
     response = "Red button";}
     if (e.target == orPossiblyMe) {
     response = "Yellow button";}
     repaint();
     return true;
     }

public void paint (Graphics g) {

     g.setColor(Color.darkGray);
     g.drawString(response, 20, 80);
}}
```

Fig. 30. Digest8 ilustrates the effect of using flow layout with offset to the right.

In *digest8* the buttons are positioned by instantiating a new flow layout, with the argument FlowLayout.RIGHT. This places them in a row at the top of the window, but offset to the right (see Fig. 30, p. 177).

Other layouts can be used, including BorderLayout, as in *digest9*.

15 Other interface components, and Action Events

Digest9 is based on a container holding three very useful components: button, check box and radio button. Another useful component, text field, is described in *digest10*.

To implement a response to user interaction with these components, use ActionListener(). There are examples in *digest7*, *digest8*, *digest9*, and *digest10*. The essentials are:

(i) Add java.awt.event.*; to the import list.

(ii) Add implements ActionListener to the class declaration.

(iii) In init(), after instantiating new components, add them to ActionListener, using:

```
nameOfComponent.addActionListener(this);
```

(iv) Set up the method to handle action events:

```
public void actionPerformed(ActionEvent e)
```

This is called automatically whenever an event occurs.

(v) This method contains the routines to identify the cause of the event, and the logic needed to take appropriate action.

Commands useful for this purpose are:

e.getSource() returns the name of the component (see digest 7).

e.getActionCommand returns the text of a label on component (*digest8*, *digest9*).

Digest9 displays some useful interface components and also demonstrates action events:

```
import java.awt.*;
import java.awt.geom.*;
import java.awt.event.*;
import javax.swing.*;

/*
<APPLET CODE=digest9 WIDTH=450 HEIGHT=200>
</APPLET>
*/
//

public class digest9 extends JApplet implements
ActionListener {

//Workbench for interface buttons, checkboxes, and
radio buttons.

    String response;
    String response1;
    String response2;
    JButton clickit;
    JCheckBox tickit;
    JRadioButton pressit;

public void init() {

    Container control = getContentPane();
    BorderLayout arrange = new BorderLayout();
    control.setLayout(arrange);

    clickit = new JButton("Click it");
    tickit = new JCheckBox("Tick it");
    pressit = new JRadioButton("Press it");
    clickit.addActionListener(this);
    tickit.addActionListener(this);
    pressit.addActionListener(this);

    control.add(clickit, BorderLayout.NORTH);
    control.add(tickit, BorderLayout.EAST);
    control.add(pressit, BorderLayout.SOUTH);
    setContentPane(control);
    control.setVisible(true);
    }

public void actionPerformed(ActionEvent e) {

    if (e.getActionCommand() == "Click it"){
    response1 = "Blue button";}
```

179

```
            else if (e.getActionCommand() == "Tick it"){
            response1 = "Red check box";}
            else if (e.getActionCommand() == "Press it") {
            response1 = "Yellow radio button";}

            if (response1 == "Red check box") {
                    if (tickit.isSelected()) {
                    response2 = " was selected";}
                    else {
                    response2 = " was deselected";}
                    }
            else if (response1 == "Yellow radio button") {
                    if (pressit.isSelected()) {
                    response2 = " was selected";}
                    else {
                    response2 = " was deselected";}
                    }
            else {response2 = " was clicked";}
            response = response1 + response2;
            repaint();
            }


    public void paint (Graphics g) {
        Graphics2D g2D = (Graphics2D)g;
        clickit.setBackground(Color.blue);
        clickit.setForeground(Color.yellow);
        tickit.setBackground(Color.red);
        tickit.setForeground(Color.black);
        pressit.setBackground(Color.yellow);
        pressit.setForeground(Color.red);

        g2D.setColor(Color.white);
        Rectangle2D.Float blankit = new
    Rectangle2D.Float(20, 65, 200, 15);
        g2D.fill(blankit);
        g2D.setColor(Color.darkGray);
        g2D.drawString(response, 20, 80);


}
```

Fig. 31 opposite shows the applet produced by Digest9. The buttons take up convenient shapes to enclose the central area of the applet. Messages and graphics can be displayed in the central area.

Clicking on the buttons is detected by the actionPerformed() method.

180

There is a similar technique for responding to mouse events:

(i) As above.

(ii) Add implements mouseListener to the class declaration or add both types of listener is required.

(iii) Use:

```
nameOfComponent.addMouseListener(this);
```

(iv) Set up **all five** mouse methods. Only those that are used need to contain routines. The others can be empty brackets { }.

See digest7A, described on p. 175, for a mouseEntered() method. The other methods required to be defined are listed on that page.

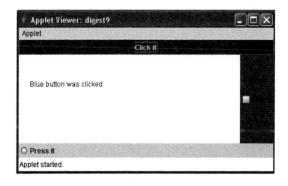

Fig. 31. In Digest9, *border layout distributes the buttons around the edges of the applet.*

More interfaces are set up in Digest10, the listing of which begins overleaf.

This program uses flow layout. Because the text field is long, no other component can be displayed at the same level. As a result the three components are displayed in a single column. The LEFT variable causes them to be lined up on the left.

```
import java.awt.*;
import java.awt.event.*;
import javax.swing.*;

/*
<APPLET CODE=digest10 WIDTH=450 HEIGHT=200>
</APPLET>
*/

public class digest10 extends JApplet implements
ActionListener {

//Workbench for labels and text fields.

     JLabel question;
     JTextField answer;
     JButton confirm;
     String response;
     boolean flag = false;

public void init() {

     Container board = getContentPane();
     FlowLayout table = new FlowLay-
out(FlowLayout.LEFT);
     board.setLayout(table);
     question = new JLabel("Which language is
best?");
     board.add(question);
     answer = new JTextField(50);
     board.add(answer);

confirm = new JButton("OK");
     board.add(confirm);
     confirm.addActionListener(this);
     setContentPane(board);
     board.setBackground(Color.green);
     board.setVisible(true);
     }

public void actionPerformed(ActionEvent e) {
     flag = false;
     if (e.getActionCommand() == "OK")
             response = answer.getText();
             response = response.toUpperCase();
     if (response.equals("JAVA")) {
             answer.setText("Correct!");
             flag = true;
             }
     repaint();
     }
```

```java
public void paint (Graphics g) {
    Graphics2D g2D = (Graphics2D)g;

    question.setForeground(Color.pink);
    answer.setBackground(Color.yellow);
    answer.setForeground(Color.red);
    confirm.setBackground(Color.blue);
    confirm.setForeground(Color.white);
    if (flag == true) {
            g2D.setColor(Color.magenta);
                        g2D.drawString(response + "
is correct!", 20, 150);
    }
} }
```

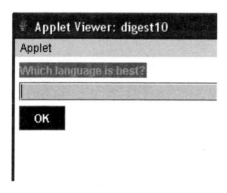

Fig. 32 Part of the applet of Digest10. *The top item, is the JLabel. Next below it is the JTextfield, which extends the whole width of the applet. Below is the OK JButton. The user clicks on this confirm that the full answer has been typed into the text field.*

16 Threads

A thread is an object that runs within a program and details a sequence of actions. Threads are used to achieve precise timing and are important in animated applets.

An example with a single thread is the *colourflash* program on p. 109. *Digest11* has three independent threads running simultaneously, to produce a traffic lights sequence.

When using threads, the class declaration must end with `implements runnable`. Then declare the thread as a global object:

`Thread    threadName = null;`

In the `start()` method, program the thread to begin running if it is not alread running (see *digest11*).

In the `stop()` method, stop the thread if it is not already stopped.

Finally, set up a `run()` method to define the action of the thread. This usually begins with a statement to check that the thread is running:

`while (threadName == Thread.currentThread(){   }`

Use separate while statements if there is more than one thread as in Digest11.

When programmming a thread, the `sleep(int)` command is used to provide a timed delay, where the int is the delay in milliseconds. A try/catch routine is used to catch an exception if the sleep if interrupted (see *digest11*). Usually, the catch() method is empty. No action is taken if an interrupt occurs.

Digest11 uses three threads

```
import java.awt.*;
import java.awt.geom.*;
import javax.swing.*;

/*
<APPLET CODE=digest11 WIDTH=60 HEIGHT=130>
</APPLET>
*/

public class digest11 extends JApplet implements
 Runnable {
```

```
//Workbench for threads.

    Thread red = null;
        Thread amber = null;
        Thread green = null;
        boolean redon = false;
        boolean amberon = false;
        boolean greenon = false;

    public void init() {

        Container screen = getContentPane();
        setContentPane(screen);
        setBackground(Color.green);
        screen.setVisible(true);
        }

    public void start() {
        if (red == null) red = new Thread(this);
        red.start();
        if (amber == null) amber = new Thread(this);
        amber.start();
        if (green == null) green = new Thread(this);
        green.start();
        }

    public void stop() {
        if (red != null) red = null;
        if (amber != null) amber = null;
        if (green != null) green = null;
        ]

 public void run() {
        while ( red == Thread.currentThread() ) {
                redon = true;
                repaint();
                try {Thread.sleep(8000); }
                catch(InterruptedException e) {}
                redon = false;
                repaint();
                try {Thread.sleep(8000); }
                catch(InterruptedException e) {}
                }

        while ( amber == Thread.currentThread() ) }
                amberon = false;
                repaint();
                try {Thread.sleep(4000); }
                catch(InterruptedException e) {}
                amberon = true;
                repaint();
                try {Thread.sleep(4000); }
                catch(InterruptedException e) {}
                }
```

```
        while ( green == Thread.currentThread() ) {
               greenon = false;
               repaint();
               try {Thread.sleep(8000); }
               catch(InterruptedException e) {}
               greenon = true;
               repaint();
               try {Thread.sleep(4000); }
               catch(InterruptedException e) {}
               greénon = false;
               repaint();
               try {Thread.sleep(4000); }
               catch(InterruptedException e) {}
               }
        }

public void paint (Graphics g) {
       Graphics2D g2D = (Graphics2D)g;

       g2D.setColor(Color.gray);
       RoundRectangle2D.Float lampholder = new
RoundRectangle2D.Float
(10F, 10F, 40F, 110F, 7F, 7F);
       g2D.fill(lampholder);
       Ellipse2D.Float redlamp = new
 Ellipse2D.Float(15F, 15F, 30F, 30F);
       Ellipse2D.Float amberlamp = new
 Ellipse2D.Float(15F, 50F, 30F, 30F);
       Ellipse2D.Float greenlamp = new
 Ellipse2D.Float(15F, 85F, 30F, 30F);

       if (redon == true) {
       g2D.setColor(Color.red);
       }
       else
       g2D.setColor(Color.darkGray);
       g2D.fill(redlamp);

       if (amberon == true) {
       g2D.setColor(Color.yellow);
       }
       else
       g2D.setColor(Color.darkGray);
       g2D.fill(amberlamp);

       if (greenon == true) {
       g2D.setColor(Color.green);
       }
       else
       g2D.setColor(Color.darkGray);
       g2D.fill(greenlamp);

       } }
```

This is a workbench program so there is scope for editing it. Change the timing of the threads to produce the sequence for traffic lights as in Australia and some other countries: red, green, amber, repeating. Change the colours of the 'lamps' and alter the timings to display new decorative sequences.

17 Java 1 versions

Chapter 4 outlined some of the advantages of working in *Java 1*, when there is no need for the advanced features of *Java 2*. This applies particularly to those getting started with applets.

Most of the listings in this book use *Java 2* commands, but there are several that are convertible to *Java 1*.

This is how to set about the conversion.

1) Normally the list of imported packages will comprise only these two:

```
import java.awt.*
import java.applet.*;
```

2) The class declaration includes 'extends applet'.

3) Delete event keywords such as ActionListener from the class declaration, Java 1 has only one event handling method and it does not need to be declared. But retain 'runnable' in the declaration.

4) In general, delete the 'J' in keywords such as JButton, JTextField, and the like.

5) Threads can be declared and the methds associated with them are retained. These include run(), start() and stop()

6) Because there are no graphics commands in the run() method, its content will be mostly unchanged.

7) The most changes will be needed in the methods that handle events and in the Graphics() method. We deal with these methods in more detail overleaf. However statements that are purely logical, including for... conditionals and while... loops are not likely to need altering.

Converting the event handling

J1 has a completely different set of methods for handling events. These are available without having to list them in the class declaration. They all return a boolean value, and the programming of the event handling method must finish with:

        return true;   or   return false;

Normally we program the event handling method to take all necessary action and, if this is so, the method finishes with return true;.

The event handling methods include:

action(Event e, Object obj)   This is used to detect an action associated with a component, such as a button. The name of the component is discovered by using the built-in 'target' variable. See examples in *moveAutoJ1* (pp. 191-192) and *cipher1J1* (pp. 192-3).

mouseDown(Event e, int, int)   The ints return the x-coordinate and y-coordinate of the cursor when the mouse button is pressed or released. Example: *catNMouseJ1* (pp. 131-136).

keyUP(Event e, int) Triggered when a key that has been pressed is released. The int equals the Unicode of the key character. Example: *validateJ1* (opposite)).

keyDown(Event e, int)   Similar action to keyUP(), but called when key is pressed.

J1 graphics

When converting a J2 program, delete the cast to g2D which always begins the paint() method. Preface g2D statements with g instead. Use the J1 versions of drawing commands as outlined on pp. 158-159 and p. 164. BasicStroke() and GeneralPath() methods are not used.

In animations and in routines where various messages are to be displayed at different times but at the same location, there may be no need to program blanking out routines. Try omitting these; J1 often clears the previous graphics automatically. An example is seen in *validateJ1* (below).

Converting to J1 may produce unintended effects. For example the textfield in *cipher1J1* has scroll-bars by default. In J2 we would have to add these by calling a special method.

J1 version of *validate*

The original *validate* is listed on pp. 101-102. Here is the J1 version, *validateJ1*:

```
import java.awt.*;
import java.applet.*;

public class validateJ1 extends Applet {

    TextField input = new TextField(10);
    int value;
    int unic;
    String message = "Key in a number (0 -9)";

public void init() {
    FlowLayout arrange = new FlowLayout();
    setLayout(arrange);
    input.setBackground(Color.yellow);
    add(input);
    setBackground(Color.cyan);
}
public boolean keyUp(Event e, int unic) {

    value = unic - 48;
    if (unic > 47 & unic < 58) message = "Key pressed
is " + value;
    else message = "Numeric keys only";
    repaint();
    return true;
}
public void paint(Graphics g) {

    g.setColor(Color.black);
    g.drawString(message, 5, 50);

}}
```

Contrast the two versions, item by item. Note how changes listed on pp. 187-188 have been made. The two versions appear to be identical.

J1 version of *bouncer*

The original version is on pp. 44-45. The J1 version is:

```java
import java.awt.*;
import java.applet.*;

public class bouncerJ1 extends Applet implements
Runnable {

     Thread moverx = null;
     Thread movery = null;
     int xDist = 50;
     int yDist = 100;
     int incx = 2;
     int incy = 1;
     Font coolFont;

public void init() {

     setBackground(Color.blue);
     Panel space = new Panel();
     add(space);
     Font coolfont = new Font("Goudy Stout",
Font.PLAIN, 20);
     setFont(coolfont);
}

public void start() {

     if (moverx == null) {
             moverx = new Thread(this);
             moverx.start();}
     if (movery == null) {
             movery = new Thread(this);
             movery.start();}
}
public void stop() {
     if (moverx != null) moverx = null;
     if (movery != null) movery = null;
     }
```

```
public void run() {
      while (moverx == Thread.currentThread()) {
            if (xDist >= 380 || xDist <= 20) {
            incx = -incx;
            }
            try
            {Thread.sleep(40);}
            catch(InterruptedException e){}
            xDist = xDist + incx;
            repaint();
            }
      while (movery == Thread.currentThread()) {
            if (yDist >= 180 || yDist <= 20) {
            incy = -incy;
            }
            try
            {Thread.sleep(60);}
                  catch(InterruptedException e){}
            yDist = yDist + incy;
            repaint();
            }}

public void paint(Graphics g) {

      g.setColor(Color.yellow);
      g.drawString("Java wins", xDist, yDist);
}}
```

As in the previous example, start(), stop() and run() are unchanged.
There is no need to blank out the previous image. so paint() is much
shorter.

J1 version of *moveAuto*

The original version is on pp. 41-42. The J1 version has the changes
specified earlier and the only major changes are in the event handler
and paint() methods. Here are the new methods:

```
public boolean action(Event e, Object obj) {
      if (e.target == startStop) {
            if (inc == 3) {
            inc = 0;}
            else if (inc == 0) {
            inc = 3;}
            }
            repaint();
            return true;
      }
```

```
public void paint(Graphics g) {
        startStop.setBackground(Color.green);
        startStop.setForeground(Color.darkGray);

        g.setColor(Color.blue);
        g.drawImage(car, xDist, 50, this);
}}
```

The action event uses the variable 'target' to find out which component generated the event. In this case it is the startstop button. Note that here it is recognised by its object name, but in the original version we identified it by its text label.

J1 version of *cipher1*

A program such as this is dealing solely with text input, processing and output. It makes no use of swing features and Gaphics2D. The same applies to the other cipher and decipher applets in Chapter 9. The J2 version is on pp. 84-86.

Few alterations are required to convert to *cipher1J1*. The import list is as on p. 84. The class declaration extends Applet, and omits ActionListener. The list of class variables is unchanged, except that we have created instances of the components here rather than in init().

There is some simplification in the init() method, which now is:

```
public void init() {
     FlowLayout arrange = new FlowLayout();
     setLayout(arrange);
     add(plainText);
     add(offset);
     add(encipher);
     cipherText.setEditable(false);
     add(cipherText);
     setBackground(Color.cyan);
```

There is no need to define a container or to specify to which interface we are adding the components. Also, we do not need to add the components to a listener method.

The start(), stop() and run() methods are unchanged, being logical.

Apart from deleting the cast to Graphics2D, the paint() method is unchanged. This is because there are no objects to draw. The commands only define the colours of the various components.

Finding the class

This is an alphabetical index to the classes described in this book.

Finding the method

A range of useful methods is decribed in the *Java Digest*. Refer to the contents list on pp.152-3.

Useful but less-often required methods are described in Part 2. These are listed below.

Notes

Notes

Notes

Notes

Notes